Colorado Madams

By Michael Rutter

FARCOUNTRY
PRESS

ISBN: 978-1-56037-773-3

Cover: Mae Phelps, photograph by Oliver E. Aultman, courtesy of History Colorado.
Back cover: Jennie Rogers, photograph courtesy of History Colorado.

For more information about our books, write Farcountry Press, P.O. Box 5630, Helena, MT 59604; call (800) 821-3874; or visit www.farcountrypress.com.

Library of Congress Cataloging-In-Publication data on file.

Produced and printed in the United States of America.

26 25 24 23 22 1 2 3 4 5

Dedication

To Shari and Abbey Rutter

Acknowledgments

A special thanks to Will Harmon, Senior Editor at Farcountry Press. A truly great editor like Will is one of the unsung heroes in the publishing world. Not only a collaborator and an advisor, Will is also a friend whose judgments I trust.

Thanks to my talented colleagues and friends, Gary Frazier, Laura Bennington-Bangerter, and Rosemary Larkin for their unselfish help on this project.

Table of Contents

The World of Colorado Madams

WE CAN NO LONGER SMELL the sweat, broken sod, and saloon sawdust, but the American West was real to those who lived it. The land was a dream, as well as a business venture for both men and women. This book tells the tales of a group of "improper" women who made their living in the Colorado boomtowns, settlements, and cities. Forget the stodgy history you memorized to pass an exam in college or learned reading Wikipedia. The Roman poet Horace taught that poetry—including stories—ought to instruct and delight. There is something charming if not magical about the dynamic world of the frontier, especially the legends, lore, and biographies of its "shady ladies."

As students of our heritage, we understand that traditional documents, pulp fiction, cultural lore, and Hollywood have not always gotten it right. Prostitution has been overly romanticized, unfairly villainized, and simply marginalized. The "soiled doves" described in song and story are more than two-dimensional prints on social wallpaper. The itinerant madam "Poker Alice" taught her whores Sunday school lessons on the Sabbath day. Bessie Rivers enjoyed photography and gardening. Laura Evens collected rococo dolls, while Lillian Powers had pets and Mattie Silks raised horses. Dora Topham, the infamous "Belle London" who may have briefly worked in Colorado, was commissioned by the Salt Lake City mayor and city council to organize "The Stockade," a block of prostitution in the downtown area, not far from the Latter-day Saints temple. Mae Phelps, like Dora Topham, championed health care for her ladies and worked with civic leaders. Mae also organized a Madams' Association.

It shouldn't be surprising that some of these women's narratives are incomplete, contradictory, or puzzling. Period newspaper accounts are very important, but it would be unwise to take what is written at face value. Objectivity and accurate reporting were not always part of the job description; a reporter's literary license could be very broad. Or, depending on the editorial posture of the paper, working women might be ignored or described euphemistically. If a woman made the news, almost never would any of the men involved be mentioned. Legal proceedings and records were inconsistent, too, since many fines and bribes were paid under the table. If you ignored shady courtesans, they were, like mosquitos, less bothersome. And yet fascinating and revealing threads and themes weave in and out of extant documents. Fair warning: the historical details sometimes peter out before these stories reach their destination, but this journey, especially in Colorado, is always worth the ride. Remember that in this profession, sporting women carefully guarded their personal information. Every discovered nit of information is a clue.

This profession holds our interest because we know it only through historical records; maybe it's akin to our fascination with the bubonic plague, Shakespeare's plays, the Salem witch trials, or serial killers. Since the "fallen women" in question are from a bygone era, their occupation may seem more benign, although the metal stays in Mollie Price's corset did turn aside a bullet, and a surly madam nicknamed "Leo the Lion" stuck a pistol dangerously close to a young Lillian Powers' face and said, "Bitch, leave town or I'll kill you."

Now that the West is embedded as an important part of American history and mythology, it's natural to look at the lives of these women through romantic or revisionist filters. Retrospection doesn't seem as sordid or deadly, especially when brothels have been turned into restaurants, travel bureaus, and historical monuments. Of course, it's even trendier if there's an unsolved murder or suggestions that a room may be haunted, as in the case of the House of Mirrors on Market Street in Denver, the Strater Hotel in Durango, and Old Homestead in Cripple Creek, to name a few.

The American experiment was certainly a socioeconomic renaissance with a global blast radius. Hardworking common folk rebelled against a stale aristocracy, embraced the responsibilities of self-governance, and drew cards in the larger game we call "the pursuit of happiness." These men and women carved out a nation based on some of the soundest ideals ever proposed. Most of what we know about bawdy women, though, is based on their professional personas. Common ladies were socially disenfranchised in their day; no one was interested in collecting their ethnographies. Socially, they existed like wallpaper or dust swept under the carpet. In California, a young schoolteacher was raped by her cousin, a businessman who was rich and powerful. Seeking child support, she was buried in a landslide of press, most of it bad. Was it possible, even in the nineteenth century, that a powerful man could ask a judge to declare his conquest insane to silence her, since she was bad for business? In Chapter 11, we'll discover what happened when she moved to Colorado and became a madam before branching into other, legitimate businesses.

Some stories are told as legends or folktales, passed down in the oral tradition. "Red Stockings" is a good example. In the early days of Leadville, she came out of nowhere—a young woman of honor stained by disgrace. It would be a luxury if we knew her real name, where she was born, or her date of birth. But in her case, folklore is all we have. Red Stockings came out of the forest like a fairy princess, associating with the first miners in the area. After a year, she left the "City in the Clouds" with bags of treasure; she changed her name, and we suppose she lived happily ever after. No records of her survive that we know of. In her day, Leadville was little more than a mining camp. And mining was a hard life, typically pursued in remote, rugged country. Miners lived in tents and ramshackle buildings; little was written down in that first phase of gold fever. What was recorded was often lost or destroyed in frequent fires.

Similarly, rumor has it that Ada Lamont was the first white woman to open her wagon tent flaps near Cherry Creek. In what would become the city of Denver, she went into business on the ground floor, so to speak. Disgraced by her preacher husband on their trip across the plains, the scorned young wife changed her name and vowed to get even. So much of her story has been built around legend, but in her instance at least we do have historical facts to give us watermarks in the midst of folklore.

These stories are fascinating and loosely historical, even if they aren't empirically verifiable. This lack of evidence may cause some professors or social scientists to roll their eyes. History belongs to us, too, and life makes good copy. It starts with stories, and this is reason enough to celebrate. This isn't an exact science; *how* it's told and *what* someone chose to say *reflects* cultural or gender values, biases, education, and social status. This includes grappling with questions of public, private, and pragmatic morality—questions we are always addressing and redefining. It's important to take a closer look at women in the West; their contributions have been largely discounted until recently. It's healthy and critical to ask new questions through different filters. This allows us to uncover a larger picture and discover voices that might otherwise have been lost.

These three crib houses were once part of Telluride's red-light district. Today, they're private homes. PHOTOGRAPH BY MICHAEL RUTTER.

This process is like putting a puzzle together and using placeholders as you try to add more to a larger mosaic. It's great when there are personal histories, family genealogies, newspaper accounts, or public records. Certainly there are inconsistencies when we look back on events or details. Consider the famous Laura Evens, a fixture in her community who closed the last days of the West and sat for interviews in her old age: we're still not completely sure if her last name is spelled Evens or Evans. Laura revealed little about her early years.

We do know that she left her husband and child and came to Colorado to start over, much like Ella Wellington, who left her husband and stepchildren, causing a scandal she could never outrun.

Managing a whorehouse was theater, as the poet T. S. Eliot would suggest, "preparing faces to meet faces." The level of the performance depended upon the price of admission. Prostitution has always been about verisimilitude, appearance, and pretense. The intensity of the illusion, the luster of the glitter, was reflected in the gate fee. After all, we expect a Broadway production to be more polished than a play at the community theater. The price of a ticket reflected a hierarchy of venues, settings, costumes, and acting. What is primarily remembered today about the Old West's "painted ladies" is their professional personas. It's like being on the front row of a good play. You see the actors' spit when they talk and the creased lines where their makeup was applied. If you're not careful, however, it's easy to get caught up in the drama because of the lighting and stagecraft and forget that a real person is playing a part. The reality was not so glamorous; the subtext was often poverty, loneliness, disease, physical abuse, and substance abuse.

Sad examples abound. Laura Bell McDaniel escaped a bad relationship. She apparently was talked into burning down her house for the insurance money by a smooth-talking man. Before it was over, the man put five bullets into another man's chest in their living room. After taking over a famous brothel in Denver, Ella Wellington had money, grace, and power, but it wasn't enough. Consider her last evening on earth: at the apex of her career, this brilliant but troubled businesswoman walked up the stairs in her opulent mansion. She turned and said to her entourage, "I'm so goddamn happy." In her bedroom she put a revolver to her temple and fired a bullet through her brains. In Cripple Creek on the night of her grand opening, another weary madam had too much to drink. Did she accidentally overdose on morphine as a sleep aid? She never woke up. Another madam, Madam Price, always seemed disagreeable. She loved to gamble and drink, but one night she couldn't stand what she saw in the mirror and quietly started taking pill after pill. When she died, no one was sorry. With few other economic opportunities, some women entered this profession to survive, but it would be very wrong to consider prostitution a charitable foundation for women. The work was driven by two important business principles: supply and demand and the bottom line. Generally, most madams weren't good at their jobs and failed. The managers who were successful—at least for a time—are the women we remember. The profession was rife with emotional and physical baggage. The world's oldest profession it may be, but rarely has the sex trade provided a sustainable livelihood. A common woman was an in-the-moment *commodity*. The nature of prostitution repeatedly consumed the players. The cast was always changing as the play itself had to change: newer houses, younger women, the next boomtown, exotic and addictive new drugs, fresh diseases, and the vagaries of aging. To top it off, the whirling social fabric and rules of engagement were in constant flux.

"The Row" in Cripple Creek was a line of two-story brothels (and single-story cribs in the background) on Myers Avenue, shown here circa 1893. They include Lola Livingston's house, Pearl Sevan's "Old Faithful," Ella Holden's "The Library," and Lottie and Kittie's "Sunnyrest." PHOTOGRAPH BY HORACE S. POLEY, COURTESY OF DENVER PUBLIC LIBRARY WESTERN HISTORY COLLECTION, L-769.

The work was far from glamorous. It was a profession of fear. Life was routinely brutal if not dangerous. There were no retirement options, and debt was part of the package. Even in a parlor house, a woman generally existed hand to mouth. The clothes were better, the food was good, the furnishings nicer, but the mantra was "live through the day." You didn't think about next week; you couldn't afford to. Besides being expelled from society and family, a common woman had few legal rights. A woman could be beaten, cheated, or raped; she could be thrown into jail or onto the street with little recourse. And worse, she rarely moved up—she moved down because hard living exacted a hard price. Suicide rates were high, substance abuse was the norm, pregnancy was always a worry, and venereal disease was a fact.

Many of the women we'll look at had high profiles, yet we know little about them. Some stepped into a national spotlight (Verona Baldwin, for example) and drew attention from the press, but still we sadly know almost nothing about them. Mollie Price, who lost a fight and part of her ear in a scuffle with another woman, died suddenly after fifteen hard years in the business. She left a healthy estate and a silent partner, presumably the silver magnate of Leadville, Horace Tabor.

A madam was running a business. Good business skills were important, but her greatest assets were interpersonal skills and long-term planning. A good number of madams died as broke as the prostitutes they employed, or they died as a result of their own bad habits. Some lived quite fast and paid dearly for their lifestyles. There were a few, though, who were crafty businesswomen; they put away nest eggs and lived comfortably in their later years. They were the exception, not the rule.

It's been well over a century since the Old West was tamed, and we cannot relive the past. But when we tell their stories, we can re-create the lives and times of these enterprising women.

By Any Other Name
Common Euphemisms

WHAT'S IN A NAME? And would a rose by any other name smell as sweet? Is a prostitute by any other name a lady?

We'll let others debate whether prostitution is the world's oldest profession. Some form of prostitution has been present in the American West at least since the beginning of Euro-American settlement. When men left families and friends to seek their fortunes and chisel out new lives in this wild land, prostitution was openly accepted and embraced. Women of "easy virtue" have been inseparably entwined with the rugged landscape and the socialization of the American West; they've also become intimately associated with the men they called clients, friends, and lovers. These so-called "daughters of joy" have been clichéd, romanticized, and castigated. As civilization established a toehold in the West, the moral atmosphere changed. Women's movements, town leaders, religious groups, and the "purity movement" fought to transform the climate of Western towns. Because prostitution was considered a threat to domestic life, the outcome of this turf war was inevitable.

It's difficult to separate fact from fiction and folklore. The cast of actors we refer to as the *demimonde* are unique and charismatic on the Western stage, even if they are elusive and coy. Their story is loud and ribald, bold and sassy, tragic and pitiful, but nevertheless important if we want an honest and accurate understanding of Western society. However, it's necessary to peel away layer after layer of strata to find the truth. There was nothing charming about the sex trade in the nineteenth century; it was an industry like any other. One professional speculated that prostitution in New Orleans was a multimillion-dollar business. Amid this booming commerce, however, there was a price tag. Thousands of working women in the Big Easy died of syphilis. How many of their clients were infected is anyone's guess.

In the West, a working woman might be known as a whore or by any of a number of colorful, if euphemistic, sobriquets: lady of the evening, prairie nymph, sporting woman, working girl, soiled dove, girl of the night, lady of the half world, and street nymph, for example. She might also be referred to as *demimondaine, nymph du pave, nymph du prairie,* and *hog.* The names of brothels were just as colorful and theatrical. A prostitute might lodge in a sporting house, bawdy house, disorderly house, cathouse, parlor house, or house of ill repute. The dwelling might also be called a parlor, social club, crib, or wine room.

A euphemism, of course, allows us to refer to something negative, troubling, difficult, or abrasive in a softer, more sanitized manner. Apparently, such phrasings help us describe disturbing, embarrassing, and painful topics—sex, war, bodily functions, love, death, race, gender—in a sensitive, socially correct fashion. For example, we don't kill our pets when they're old or ill, we put them to sleep. Family members don't die, they pass on. Wild young boys don't commit crimes, they get sideways of the law. Cultured people don't get gonorrhea, they contract a social disease. Seemingly colorful names given to prostitutes, and the names prostitutes called themselves, are more telling than they might first appear.

What does Gertrude Stein's famous line mean: "A rose is a rose is a rose"?

What's in a name? Apparently, a whore by any other name is still a whore. Let's take a look at some of the colorful prostitution euphemisms used in the West and consider what they tell us about gender, cultural values, and societal norms.

Alley cat	A prostitute. Ladies of the evening were frequently called cats, and many houses were in alleys. See cathouse.
Bagnio	A place of prostitution, brothel, bordello, bawdy house.
Bawd	A prostitute, a woman of easy virtue. From Middle English meaning lively and bold, commonly in an immoral way.

Bawdy house A brothel or bordello. From bawdy, sexual, off color.

Belladonna A prostitute. Women sometimes used the poison plant belladonna to dilate their eyes to appear more attractive.

Black-eyed Susan A prostitute, usually referring to a girl of color—most often an African American, but also including Mexicans and Indians.

Boarder A prostitute at a "boardinghouse" (see below). Some thought the term gave them respectability since it implied that they paid rent.

Boardinghouse A place of prostitution. The term implied a semblance of respectability since boarders paid "rent."

Bordello A place of prostitution. From Old French meaning hut or small house.

Brothel A place of prostitution.

Calico A prostitute, likely taken from calico cat since prostitutes were frequently called cats.

Cat A prostitute, perhaps having something to do with moodiness, independence, or nine lives.

Cathouse A place of prostitution, home of the "cats."

Caught, Getting A prostitute's term for getting pregnant.

Ceremonial husband A man who marries a prostitute for practical, business reasons, perhaps to be her pimp. He may or may not live with her.

Colored Susan A prostitute of color, usually African American but might be Mexican or Indian.

Common woman A prostitute, whom anyone could have for a price.

Cottage A prostitute's shack or cabin was often referred to as a cottage. It was usually small with one or two rooms, cheaply constructed, but a little larger and sometimes better built than a crib.

Cottage girl A prostitute who lived and worked in her cottage.

Courtesan A prostitute, a highly paid woman who associated with the wealthy, a woman who sold her favors to only one or two men.

Crib A small room, cheaply constructed, where a lower-class prostitute lived and did business.

Crib girl A low-class prostitute who worked in a crib house, but not always.

Crib house A group of crib-like, small, shabby, cheap apartments in red-light district housing.

Daughter of sin A prostitute. Like Eve, daughters of sin used their charms to lead men astray.

Daughter of Venus A prostitute, referring to the Roman goddess of love.

Demimonde A French term for the half-world, used to describe the shadowy world of prostitution and the shady women who sold their bodies. The term was coined from Alexandre Dumas' play, *Le Demi-Monde*, published in 1855.

Demi-monde *Demimonde*, frontier spelling.

Denizen A prostitute or place of prostitution.

Disorderly girl/woman A prostitute, called a disorderly girl because of the disorderly business she was involved in.

Disorderly house	A place of prostitution, called disorderly because of the wicked, disorderly business that took place there.
Dive	A place of prostitution, one that is tawdry and lower class, a place where a man might get cheated or robbed.
Dove	A prostitute. Short for soiled dove.
Fair sister	A prostitute, a weaker vessel like Eve, inclined to fall morally.
Fallen	A prostitute, referring to Eve's fall. More specifcally a girl who had come from a respectable family or had fallen from her former religious beliefs.
Fancy woman	A prostitute, probably meaning one who dressed to attract attention and put herself in a better light.
Fille de joie	A prostitute, French for a "girl of joy."
Frail sister	A prostitute, referring to the belief that only a weak, morally frail woman would enter this profession.
Half Acre	A shortened version of Hell's Half Acre, a red-light district.
Harlot	A prostitute. From the Middle English meaning itinerate, vagabond.
Harpy	A prostitute. From a loathsome, voracious monster in Greek mythology with a woman's head and trunk.
Harridan	A very disagreeable prostitute, a scolding, vicious woman who is worn out.
Haute couture	A well-dressed prostitute, a parlor girl.
Hell's Half Acre	A red-light district, a place owned by the devil, sometimes the specific name of a house. Both Fort Worth and San Antonio, Texas, had infamous districts called Hell's Half Acre.

Hog	A low-class, worn-out prostitute who works at a hog ranch (see below), where men weren't very particular and women were cheap.
Hog ranch	A place of prostitution, generally near a military post.
Hooker	A prostitute, named after the working girls who followed General Hooker's troops during the Civil War.
House of ill repute	A place of prostitution. Both the women and the men who visited them were considered to be of ill repute and debasing themselves.
House of inmates	A place of prostitution. Prostitution was, at the least, a metaphoric, moral prison.
House of Magdalene	A place of prostitution named after Mary Magdalene, who some believe was a reformed prostitute.
House of Queens	A place of prostitution named after the women who were ironically referred to as "queens," perhaps queens of sin.
Inmate	A prostitute. A prostitute was a social, if not actual, prisoner of her profession.
Lady of the evening/night	A prostitute, so-called because in her profession she worked mostly evenings.
Lady of the half world	A prostitute. When a woman entered into the sisterhood of prostitution she could no longer claim the "decent" world; thus, she lived in a half or shadow world.
Laundress	A low-class prostitute.

Lewd	A prostitute, because of her immoral action.
Lewd house	A place of prostitution, because of immoral actions that occurred there.
Line	A red-light district. A person might go to the line or work on the line.
Magdalene	A prostitute, taken from Mary Magdalene, the repentant sinner who some believed was a reformed prostitute.
Mother	A madam who was kind to her girls, who was a surrogate mother to her boarders.
Nun	Derogatory term referring to a woman of questionable virtue. Dating from at least the Middle Ages.
Nunnery	A derogatory term for a place of prostitution, dating from at least the Middle Ages. In Shakespeare's play, Hamlet told Ophelia to "get thee to a nunnery," meaning go to a whorehouse and become a whore.
Nymph	A prostitute, a term rooted in Greek and Roman mythology.
Nymph du pave	A prostitute. French for "lady of the pavement" or street; literally one who walked the street, although it came to mean any hooker.
Painted lady	A prostitute who paints her face. Many prostitutes wore a lot of makeup, which was shocking to "decent" women. In the early days, makeup might have been used to mask a woman's true identity.

Parlor house	A place of prostitution, the finest establishment where the girls were pretty, the food and wine excellent, and the game of romance was superficially played.
Prairie flower	A prostitute.
Prairie nymph	A prostitute.
Public house	A place of prostitution, called public since anyone with money could "know" the women who worked inside; what she should have kept private she made public, for a price.
Queen	A prostitute, a common name for a brothel girl.
Red-light district	An area of prostitution containing more than one brothel.
The Row	A red-light district, an area with a number of brothels or cribs. Probably named "Row" because flesh purveyors or crib houses were often stacked side by side on a street or alley (Holladay Street in Denver, for example).
Row girl	A prostitute.
Seminary	A place of prostitution. Ironic religious reference to ungodly women and actions.
Shady lady	A woman who hid physically and morally in the shadows during the day and came out at night to ply her trade.
Shanty	A cheaply constructed shack or house used for prostitution.

Sister/ Sisterhood	The profession of prostitution. A woman forsook all that was decent when entering the profession; all she had left were her fellow sisters in sin.
Social club	A place of prostitution, usually a higher-class establishment.
Soiled dove	A prostitute, a pure woman who let herself get defiled by sin and misery.
Sporting house	A place of prostitution.
Sporting section	A place of prostitution, a district of prostitution, a place where sporting women gathered.
Sporting woman	A prostitute.
Street nymph	A prostitute who walked the street, a streetwalker.
Streetwalker	The bottom of the rung among prostitutes, a woman who walked the street to find clients.
Summer vacation	When a madam loaded up her girls and took them to a mining area, cow town, army base, railhead, or cattle drive for extra business.
Tenderloin	A red-light district, an especially corrupt area.
Unfortunate one	A euphemism often used in publications, frequently when a prostitute died or committed suicide.
Upstairs girl	A prostitute. Most brothels were located on a second story for privacy, security, and protection.
Upstairs house	A place of prostitution. Most prostitutes were housed on the second story (see upstairs girl).

Wayward sister	A prostitute, probably coined because she was considered to have lost her way morally.
Whore	A prostitute, ironically from the root "desired woman."
Wine room	A place of prostitution with a room where clients could drink different wines.

1

Ada Lamont

The Legend of the Young Bride, the Whore, and the Madam

THEY CALLED THE PLACE "INDIAN ROW," but one day it would become known as Denver. A recent arrival—a pretty girl in her late teens—told settlers that anyone looking for a good time would find her "available" under a new name, Ada Lamont. "As of tomorrow," she proclaimed, "I'll start a brothel in this settlement." She didn't have to say it twice. In a land hungry for women, Ada found a ready market.

Her minister husband had disgraced her, apparently running off with another woman. Ada had thought she'd be dedicating her life to the service of God, but instead she found herself alone in the West, at a crossroads in her life. Though disillusioned, like a character from a Katherine Anne Porter short story, she was not without a plan.

That plan was to become the first White woman to sell herself in the settlement. Intimate with some of the town's most successful men, her business scaled rapidly, and she managed it well—for a time. Maybe she pushed too hard, maybe she took shortcuts, or maybe life pushed back. She was a bold woman in a new land. Did drink, fast living, or poor choices catch up with her? Or was her life an Old West correlative of a Greek tragedy?

Fate managed to catch her off guard a second time. The prosperous Ada learned that her husband might not have deserted her after all. The stuff of legends—like Oedipus—it seems that Ada couldn't escape what she'd done or the will of the gods. Blinded by despair and cheap whiskey, the first courtesan of Colorado lost everything. Reduced to homelessness and despair, she would end up starving to death on the streets of Georgetown, Colorado, during the peak of the silver boom. Was her story real or the yarning of morality-driven campfire tales?

In 1858, Ada and her husband set off to what they hoped would be the land of milk and honey. Maybe they wrote "Pikes Peak or Bust" on the side of their wagon. Over 100,000 people would flock to the newest El Dorado in the Rocky Mountains; newspaper headlines said the migrants had "Yellow Fever." In the wake of the Panic of 1857, glowing accounts of "easy pickings" and "unbelievable wealth" fueled hopes of ready riches.

Fevered East Coast adventurers flocked to Missouri. The first step on their journey was to find a wagon train going to the Rocky Mountains. The second step was to cross the plains as quickly as possible. The third was to pick up nuggets the size of your fist. However, this young missionary couple's stairway to heaven wouldn't glitter with gold but rather with the souls they won for the kingdom of God.

The hard lessons of the past twenty years were conveniently absent from the hyperbolic headlines and articles of the day. Promised lands are never reached without a body count along the way—the California Gold Rush, Mormon pioneers, and Oregon Trail come to mind. The mythic goldfields of Colorado would be no different. Some got "busted" after they got to the Rocky Mountains. Others "busted" on the plains.

The details of Ada's life are scarce; we don't even know her real name. But we can put some of the pieces together. By all outward signs, Ada's life was one of great expectations. She came from a good family and was educated. They say her groom was a fine-looking man—a man of the cloth. Ada was a tall, quiet girl. She was more

The August 13, 1859, issue of Harper's Weekly *carried an article extolling the pioneers "Crossing the Plains" to seek their fortunes in the Pikes Peak gold mines. The accompanying illustrations, including this one, painted a less rosy picture.* ILLUSTRATION COURTESY OF THE LIBRARY OF CONGRESS, LC-USZ62-72001.

striking than beautiful and was considered introspective. She brooded about knowing the will of God because she wanted to live a Christian life. The couple's future was one of hope. They were yoked equally in their shared commitment to their union, the service of mankind, and the service of God.

The story at this point gets tangled. According to folklore, Ada was a newly wedded bride when she crossed the dusty plains. That makes a good story, but it's more likely she'd been married for a year or two by then, so they weren't actual newlyweds.

Nevertheless, they were drawn by the promise of a better future on the wild frontier. A mining town in the Territory of Kansas would be their mission; this territory stretched from the western border of Missouri to the middle of the Rocky Mountains. They would minister to wandering, wavering souls and would baptize and save as many "heathen" Indians as they could. Later, when the women and children came, they would start a proper church and build a city on a hill, a Zion, like Enoch in the Old Testament.

Like all proverbial and proper missionaries, they were poor and willing to live on faith. With what they'd saved and with "love offerings" from the laity, they had enough to outfit a wagon to cross the country to the eastern slope of the Rockies. More importantly, they had each other. They understood that the trek across the Great Plains wasn't without peril. Undoubtedly, the couple was nervous as they started on the overland trail. Regardless of the hyperbolic headlines about the new El Dorado, it was a dangerous adventure. The trail guides were misleading, if not fallacious. Other dangers included buffalo stampedes, precarious weather, cholera, typhoid, starvation, and fatal accidents. Perhaps most troubling was the unending fear of Indian attacks.

One night after a long, monotonous day on the trail, after Ada had picked up her share of buffalo chips for the evening fire, her husband did not return. Presumably, he'd been grazing the livestock or hunting. Ada naturally thought the worst. Had savages attacked him? Had a snake bitten him? Did his horse throw him? Where was he? The wagon train mounted a search and even nervously camped for a second precious day—always fearing "the war party" rumored to be in the area. The men looked in vain, knowing they must move on.

By the end of the second day, someone had put some pieces together. Suspiciously, a certain young woman of the party appeared to be missing, too. She was suspected of having questionable morals. The thinking was that this "Jezebel" had somehow tempted the good minister with pleasures of the flesh, he had fallen, and they'd run off. This was convenient. It made it easier for the men to call off the search so the train could move out of dangerous territory.

Deserted, Ada was crushed and overwhelmed. It was understandably difficult for those who had to break the news to her. Her first fears had been his murder, injury, capture, or torture. As awful as this anxiety had been, it didn't wound her as deeply as the personal betrayal she was now experiencing. As her shame grew, she kept to herself. Her grief festered into bitterness—and then into a full-blown crisis of faith. She might have considered it her foreordained duty to go to the goldfields as a widowed missionary and do the work her husband had wanted to begin. But his infidelity stung her to the core. She questioned her values and wondered if her life had been built on a lie. She'd been betrayed by the sins of the flesh. If men were so weak, she reckoned, one could profit by it. She might also have realized that, with no husband, she needed to support herself in the new land. As an educated, bright young woman, she had options other women might not have had. Somehow, becoming a whore seemed the best way to get back at the man and the theology that had forsaken her. Her new mission statement became: get even and prosper from original sin. By the time the wagons reached Cherry Creek, she had come out of isolation and redefined her world. In wording as tight as an Emily Dickinson poem, she stated to the world, "As a God-fearing woman, you see me for the last time. As of tomorrow, I will start the first brothel in this settlement. Come have some fun."

For Ada, there was no time like the present to open a new business—a business she ran behind the canvas flaps of her wagon until a permanent structure could be built. For the only prostitute in a sea of lonely, unchaperoned men, there was money to be made. Business thrived, and she expanded. Within a year, Ada opened a fancy parlor house on Arapahoe Street. She offered the best liquor, food, and women that money could buy, all freighted across the plains. The ex-preacher's wife now tended another kind of flock, and (it was said) she was her brother's keeper. In her new role, she associated professionally and personally with the early movers and shakers of the region. Her establishment became a natural gathering place for men to take business before pleasure.

Shown here in 1864 at the intersection of 15th and Arapahoe Streets, Denver was little more than a small town with a big future. PHOTOGRAPH BY WILLIAM GUNNISON CHAMBERLAIN, COURTESY OF DENVER PUBLIC LIBRARY, WESTERN HISTORY COLLECTION, X-22031.

Ada was a party girl for hire, comfortable with speculators, miners, and freighters. She had answers to any man's questions if he paid in gold. A wonderful collection of tales has been woven around Ada. They include some of the more nefarious characters on the eastern slope of the Rockies. In 1859, she met a gambler and shifty businessman named Charlie Harrison but known as "Forty-Niner." They became good friends. He was in his early forties and smartly dressed. He sported a well-groomed beard and stood out from the usual clientele, who frequently wore homespun or canvas pants. Ada was barely twenty when they met, but the two became a pair.

Harrison, like Ada, is also steeped in Western folklore. It's difficult to sift facts from folklore, but the stories are good and fact-checking was never a strong suit with frontier newspapermen or storytellers. We know that Harrison was friendly and affable, but he could be hot-tempered and handy with his pearl-handled, cap-and-ball Colt .45 pistols. He seemed to get into a fair amount of trouble in the two years he was in Denver. He proved he was willing to shoot his way out of said trouble, or simply shoot if he was so inclined.

Some of the details of this duo's story are real; others aspects are fabricated. But they made good copy in the papers. As with Bonnie and Clyde or the Sundance Kid and Etta Place, we love the oft-told tales of a doomed, fallen woman—with a tragically cloaked past—and her misunderstood, moody gunman lover. Embellishment and bravado were good for business for both gamblers and madams. It didn't matter what people said, as long as they talked about you.

Denver was a wild town in its early days. Men were rough, unrefined, and proud of it. Fortunes were made and lost overnight. Whiskey was gulped like water, and while a whorehouse was a whorehouse, it was also a place where men conducted affairs of government, blew off steam, and socialized.

It was said that Harrison had notched his six-guns, fought Mormons, belonged to the Masons, and promoted horse races. Like other gunmen, he was credited with more shootings than he actually committed. And while Ada was a fallen woman, she had a reputation for running an honest house, where a man who drank too much didn't need to worry about being robbed if he hired one of Ada's girls. Just as important, she didn't water down the drinks.

The pair apparently had a working and personal reciprocity. They covered each other's backs and for a time were leaders in their respective underworlds. They caroused among the well-heeled and did good business with both greenhorns and seasoned prospectors. When Charlie came to town, he worked at the Denver House saloon, running a monte game. However, he soon bought a saloon called the Criterion. His watering hole became the center of his activities as he expanded his interests. Ada and Charlie were often seen together, throwing parties and going to parties in their own establishments or in one of the thirty other saloons in Denver. Being associated with a so-called tough guy like Charlie was a good business move for Ada. Few men would cause a disturbance in her house while she enjoyed his favor.

On the eve of the Civil War, loyalties in the territory were split, old friends were divided, and conflict seemed likely. Harrison, an outspoken Southerner, was involved in more than one serious skirmish. We have no idea what Ada's politics were. For a time, it looked as if she stood by her man. Ada might have cared on some level for her rebel, but she was likely more concerned with the color of a man's gold than his loyalties to the blue or the gray. Or maybe she was in love with Harrison; she would commit crimes for her friend.

Both were quickly caught in a frenetic maelstrom of newspaper articles and polarizing public opinions. Newton Byers of the *Rocky Mountain News* wrote critical pieces about Harrison and his gang. Charlie had been bold, outspoken, and pushy. He was edgy, looking for a fight to prove his loyalty to the Confederate cause. A Black gambler named Stark provided the opportunity he was looking for. Stark insulted Charlie's Southern honor by not showing him enough respect; the gambler had made the fatal mistake of addressing Charlie by his first name. As Harrison saw it, the freed Black man didn't know his place. Harrison had no other choice but to shoot him dead with one of his fancy Colts. He balanced the scales—and he bragged about it. Later, he would say Stark came at him with a Bowie knife, so he shot in self-defense. Meanwhile, Harrison was arrested, indicted for murder, and tried. The good-hearted madam did what she could. It was said that she bribed the jurors with $5,000 in cash to make sure Charlie went free. Other legends have her threatening jury members with physical harm or offering her house's "favors," along with fine bottles of wine. It's a buffet of possibilities. Choose your favorite.

Later, at the Criterion, there was a shootout between Union and Confederate sympathizers. Some say the disagreement started at Ada's parlor house. Harrison had the support of the mayor, John C. Moore, who was also a Southerner and ran interference. In due time, Charlie got into more serious legal trouble, shooting a rancher in a duel and causing further disruptions. Civic leaders wondered if there was a way to make him go away so they could do business in peace. They didn't need a martyr for the South.

By this time, Ada and Charlie were having serious public fights. Apparently, these were over a floozy named Lizzie Greer, a blonde who drank too much and had set her cap for Harrison.

Facing a murder charge, Charlie accepted a plea deal. Presumably, he had Ada's help; either she wanted to get rid of him or they'd patched things up. Ada paid a rather large fine, and Harrison signed a loyalty oath to the United States and promised to leave Colorado and never return. The oath of loyalty was quickly forgotten, however. Realizing he could do more for the cause than stir up contention in a frontier town, Harrison accepted an officer's commission in the Confederacy. By most accounts, he turned into a good soldier. The glib frontier grifter was promoted and commended for his leadership and valor in battle. He had at last found a cause. He fought in a number of battles. Once, he led a group of soldiers to disrupt and loot critical Union supply lines. Later, out on the plains, he ran into a band of Osage Indians and was killed.

In the meantime, Ada was apparently glad to get rid of him. She prospered. There's no record that she or Harrison contacted each other—or cared to. She moved on and plied her trade. Denver prospered during the war. Competition was keen, and Ada wasn't getting any younger in a profession that was never kind to maturity. But she was established and doing well.

The next part of Ada's story unfolded quickly. The tale seems neatly manipulated for effect. Some parts are biographical, but the retelling has been crafted into a morality tale. It's likely the embodiment of several frontier legends mixed into one story to teach a lesson.

The successful Ada started to feel plagued again by the disappearance of her husband. The money, her new life, and revenge weren't as sweet as she'd hoped. In her quiet hours when she took her makeup off, when the buzz from wine and whiskey wore off, she was haunted by ghosts of what might have been. Her thoughts drifted back to her husband and their life together. She began wondering what had really happened to her ill-fated minister husband.

Again, we must remember that Ada's story is a good story, but it feels managed. It's said that, in the midst of her doubts, a friend planned to travel back East. On his journey, he came across a skull with a jagged bullet hole on the plains of Kansas. More importantly, he found a Bible near the remains, with an inscription from none other than Ada. He also discovered other cherished keepsakes from—you guessed it—the then-young bride. It's possible this wasn't Ada's husband, but so is winning millions in the lottery.

Knowing Ada's story, the man rapidly conducted his business and made his way back to Denver to tell his madam friend what he'd found and to give her the Bible she'd given her beloved husband on their wedding day. He must have been a good friend, because most people knew her as Ada Lamont. That's not the name she would have written in the Bible. (This is but one of many loose ends that makes the story seem too good to be true.)

And so, the story goes, Ada realized that she hadn't been jilted after all. Her faith in the man she loved had been real. Her subsequent life had been a sham. We can almost feel the crafter of the tale saying, "And now, gentle reader, the fallen madam, like King David, Oedipus, King Lear, and Mother Eve, feels she's beyond redemption. Indians killed her love! He had kept the Bible she'd given him. He didn't run off with a wagon-train floozy. In the end, it was she who had proved faithless as she paved her way to hell on a downward spiral, committing the wickedest of immoralities. Disillusioned, the forlorn Ada drowned herself in drink and tumbled into depression.

Not caring about anything, she lost her business, boarded up her whore house, and became a streetwalker. She died in gin-soaked obscurity from starvation.

What do we really know about Ada Lamont? She was a young woman who crossed the Great Plains and ran a successful brothel in Colorado. She was part of a wild crowd that included Charlie Harrison. She lived fast, drank too much, lost her business, and tragically died on the streets of Georgetown. Beyond that, it's hard to say which details are factual history and which are merely story. ൟ

JANE BOWEN

The Sage Hen Was the First Lady of Blair Street

THEY CALLED HER THE "SAGE HEN." They called her "Aunt Jane." Her married name was Jane Bowen, and she ran the first full-time brothel in a boomtown that was out of control even by boomtown standards. Jane was from London, England. She and her husband, William, opened Winchester Hall on Greene Street in Silverton. It was a dance hall, variety theater, saloon, and brothel. People called it the Sage Hen's Dance Hall.

The Bowens were involved in a number of business ventures in Silverton and became quite wealthy. They soon built a large home and another brothel. The wild town served their interests; they catered to the vices. However, William also owned interests in a number of mining shares.

In Silverton, you lived hard, played hard, and died hard. It was the sort of town you wouldn't take your mother to because you went there to make money and live like the prodigal son. Most men arrived broke and left broke. The city fathers called in Bat Masterson, the gunfighter, to help tame the wildness. Shootings and robberies were commonplace, and vice ran uncontrolled. The town set its clock by shifts at the mine and ran twenty-four hours a day. Depending on who was counting, there were thirty-two brothels, forty saloons, and thirty gambling houses. The bawdy ladies, the newspaper reported, were so vulgar that they offended some miners.

Silverton was incorporated in 1874. At 9,400 feet above sea level, the only way in was by a precarious "wagon trail" that required a block and tackle—and steel nerves. Travelers had to cross Stony Pass, which tops out at over 12,000 feet and is called Stony for a reason. Besides silver, the local economy centered around whiskey, women, and wagering. In one of Jane's businesses, called The Laundry, it was said that "if you came in with any money, you came out clean."

But the miners were accustomed to taking risks. Blasting mistakes, avalanches, cave-ins, disease, and almost random violence all took a toll. Men were valued less than ore and livestock.

In the 1880s, William became sick with consumption. He deeded his estate to his wife before he died. Jane continued to do business and raise their adopted daughter. Jane moved in and out of various business ventures, including the Palace Hall in 1892. She threw lavish balls that the entire town attended. But life for Aunt Jane had its share of tragedies. Her daughter killed herself with rat poison at the age of twenty-eight. One of Jane's nephews from England died mysteriously after arriving in Silverton, and another tried to poison her with carbolic acid after an argument. Jane's nerves were frazzled, so she took a long vacation to England in 1898 to get away from her troubles. She leased out her property while she was gone.

In 1902, she returned and resumed management of her dance hall, but her heart was no longer in the brothel business and she retired in 1905.

2

Red Stockings

The Myth, the Legend, the Miner's Dream Girl

IN 1860, IT WAS A BEAUTIFUL MOUNTAIN VALLEY—soon to be called the "City in the Clouds." At 10,152 feet above sea level, in the shadow of Mount Elbert, the second-highest peak in the continental United States, you did your best to stay warm. But mostly you looked for gold. We know the area today as Leadville, Colorado.

It was a lonely country when Abe Lee struck pay dirt. He said, "I've got all of California in my pan," so he called his strike California Gulch. By summer's end, perhaps 10,000 feverish miners swarmed the alpine valley like frenetic bees to tender wildflowers.

Like a fairy-tale Snow White, Red Stockings came out of the dark forest and took care of her miners. She was pretty—shapely, trim, and ample. Her skin was as white as fresh snow and her cupid-bow lips were as red as blood. Her cocoa eyes and pitch-black hair (tied with red ribbons) were the stuff of dreams on frigid nights. Her elfin smile—one of her trademarks—was bewitching. Miners thrilled if they caught a glimpse of her famous red socks or her ankles. So desperate were they to see a woman, they might have waited for hours, hoping she would ride by on her horse that afternoon. Then they would clap and cheer. They said she would turn and smile—not the way a whore smiles, but the way a real woman smiles, like someone you've known for a long time and wished you could make your own. You'd give anything, pay anything, to be with her.

Of course, being one of the first women in a camp of lonely men was a distinct marketing advantage. Did she tell someone her real name? If she did, no one remembers it. She was an overnight legend. In less than a year, this log-cabin courtesan with thick red socks had found what she was looking for: a way out, a strike of her own. She made enough money to live like a princess, happily ever after.

The miners talked about a farewell party their lady gave, when pack trains brought the best liquor into camp. It was her going-away present for the good-hearted men who had treated her so kindly. They made her retirement—about $100,000 (today, $3 million, tax-free)—possible. It was one last celebration—her graduation party—and then she'd go, as she must, and never come back. The men respected her decision but were sorry.

She had a small cabin and possibly a few other ladies helping her, but there was something different about this woman—you could never forget her.

The story of Red Stockings is a curious mixture of Snow White, Disney's *Mulan*, Goethe's *Faust*, and a variation on the song "The Devil Went Down to Georgia." As her judge and jury, the Leadville gold miners "saved" her in their mythological lore. They gave her a nobility, a dignity, usually reserved for tragic heroes in epic literature. Her legend is an American morality tale.

A sage elderly miner, remembering the early days, said, "When ya make a *gutshot* straight on the largest pot of your life, cash out, leave the table, and never play poker again." As we explore the legend

This image of Oro City at the foot of California Gulch, which was eventually subsumed by Leadville, gives a sense of the valley's quiet charm before the silver boom. PHOTOGRAPH BY CLARENCE RECKMEYER, COURTESY OF HISTORY COLORADO, CHS.X4663.

of Red Stockings, remember we're looking at a real person, but no formal records survive. Others can worry about the abstractions of historical accuracy, or the lack thereof; this is a delightful story. In our world of political correctness, we should never become too sophisticated to delight in a mountain flower or a folktale for its own sake. We appreciate the journalist Maxwell Scott who, in the classic John Ford Western film *The Man Who Shot Liberty Valance,* said, "This is the West, sir. When the legend becomes fact, print the legend."

The men around California Gulch said Red had a mysterious past, although they didn't talk about it loudly. Some thought she'd come from the East—maybe Boston—where her father was an important businessman. The lady had manners, education, and class. There were whispers about her being married or keeping company with a nobleman from Europe, possibly a gambler. As dignified as a princess, she had a common touch. One oft-repeated but apocryphal account ran, "Damnit if she wasn't assigned to purgatory, but that woman kept her head up as she done her penance. Took it like a man, she did, like a man. Then she got out—didn't ask for pity." People talked of how she changed her name and started a new life as an honest woman. She married someone who loved her back. The miners said the couple built a ranch together and had kids. Some said it was in Nevada, but no, maybe . . . hell, was it California? They said she lived happily ever after. She was proof that a lowly commoner, like a cinder girl, could still marry a prince—or better yet, win against long odds, become rich, and choose someone to marry.

In the nineteenth century, the existence of shady ladies was swept under the rug, so the truth needs to be unraveled wherever it is found. History is mostly written by the winners, so it's helpful to revisit the past with different filters or perspectives. It's healthy to challenge or reexamine some of the original assumptions, but if we don't enjoy the ride, we're missing something.

Nevertheless, we can learn a great deal by unpacking Red's myth. To start, Red's champions, the miners, didn't look at her the way they would have looked at Mattie Silks, Jennie Rogers, or Laura Evens—other soiled doves. In fancy terms, Red was not a *contrasexual stereotype*; she wasn't seen as a woman who defied the moral norms of the nineteenth century, specifically the societal norms such as the "Cult of True Womanhood" or "Cult of Domesticity." Mattie, Jennie, and Laura were neither submissive, pious, nor domestic. They were defiant, haughty, childless, single, independent, and exploitive, openly displaying their sexuality.

Today, we might see these madams as entrepreneurs or likable tricksters, perhaps a bit gilded and tarnished. We might even suggest that they represent gender inequality or an economic class struggle. However, in their day, they were soiled doves, the fallen Eves. They would thank the serpent in the Garden of Eden, devour the forbidden fruit, and walk out of paradise with a wicked smile, figuring ways to monetize their charms in a fallen world.

Red Stockings, on the other hand (at least in the common telling), wasn't an exploiter. She was a social casualty. She represented a fallen innocent within an unduly harsh moral tradition. As she struggled with conflicting ideologies and her plight, her only choice was self-imposed banishment. Unlike Mary, the Mother of God, she had no Joseph, no kindly man who refused to make a public spectacle of her. Red Stockings faced the whims of social circumstances and wouldn't dishonor her family.

Her character had a contemporary feel, as if she had stepped out of a play by Eugene O'Neill. If you've read Herman Melville's novella

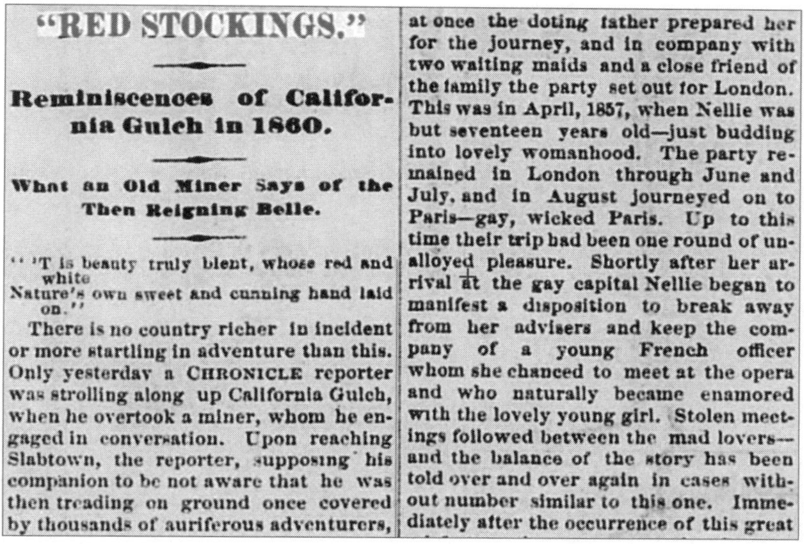

"RED STOCKINGS."

Reminiscences of California Gulch in 1860.

What an Old Miner Says of the Then Reigning Belle.

"'T is beauty truly blent, whose red and white
Nature's own sweet and cunning hand laid on."

There is no country richer in incident or more startling in adventure than this. Only yesterday a CHRONICLE reporter was strolling along up California Gulch, when he overtook a miner, whom he engaged in conversation. Upon reaching Slabtown, the reporter, supposing his companion to be not aware that he was then treading on ground once covered by thousands of auriferous adventurers,

at once the doting father prepared her for the journey, and in company with two waiting maids and a close friend of the family the party set out for London. This was in April, 1857, when Nellie was but seventeen years old—just budding into lovely womanhood. The party remained in London through June and July, and in August journeyed on to Paris—gay, wicked Paris. Up to this time their trip had been one round of unalloyed pleasure. Shortly after her arrival at the gay capital Nellie began to manifest a disposition to break away from her advisers and keep the company of a young French officer whom she chanced to meet at the opera and who naturally became enamored with the lovely young girl. Stolen meetings followed between the mad lovers—and the balance of the story has been told over and over again in cases without number similar to this one. Immediately after the occurrence of this great

The April 16, 1879, edition of the Leadville Daily Chronicle *featured the legend of Red Stockings.*
IMAGE COURTESY OF THE COLORADO HISTORIC NEWSPAPERS COLLECTION.

Billy Budd, Red was what we might call a Billy Budd–style character; she represented innocence steamrolled by the system.

Thankfully, Red's final judge wouldn't be a wicked stepmother who wanted to destroy her or a familial social structure bent on expelling her. The miners, like the dwarfs, embraced her feminine presence in their male world. As a result, her legend manifests several fascinating core patterns or archetypes. Like any good tale, over time her allegorical sketch reinvents itself with new twists, giving it a new life. The most important message, though, is that Red Stockings—the beloved, common camp woman—found redemption, a chance to start over.

While she was certainly a real woman, Red also represents, through mythology, several important allegorical elements. Because of this, the *impact* of her story is as important as the story itself. As a "dishonored" young woman, she fled to protect her family's good name before it was vilified. The prospectors understood this was how it was and had to be, even if it didn't seem fair. Her scenario was all too common, especially back East, in the civilized world the miners had left. On the frontier, perspectives shifted. Everything was scarce, especially whiskey and women. Red had likely been disgraced for an unspecified sexual situation. Sin, shame, disgrace, disinheritance, and then prostitution were inevitable steps in the freefall to hell.

However, to the miners, this was wasteful. What sense did it make to cast off a perfectly good and valuable woman because of a black-and-white morality? And who would cast the first stone when standing inside a whorehouse?

Prostitution was considered a deal with the devil; it was about as low as a woman could fall. Red somehow outwitted Old Scratch and got out with her fortune and her soul. She wasn't greedy, since she could've held out for more. Getting out of the goldfields rich, of course, was also the miner's dream. John Morse, the fiery editor of the Sacramento *Daily Union*, summed up the miner's vision nearly a decade earlier: "I came to this country to make money, make the most amount of money in the shortest possible time, out of the least capital . . . put money in thy purse, honestly if thou canst, but put money in thy purse." (*Daily Union*, March 20, 1851).

Yes, Red Stockings had "done wrong, but who hasn't," the miners would say. At the same time, they also took a good-natured jab at the hypocritical double standard that some of the rough men understood was their civilized alter ego.

Red was one of the imaginative mental opiates that lonely men turned to when there was no campfire or whiskey to keep them warm. This woman came out of the forest like a goddess, like Snow White, motivating them to get up in frigid darkness, make a fire to combat the cold, eat bad food, and search for the elusive fortune that would set them free. Like a good dream, they could think about her during the day, too, a frontier version of *everywoman*. The miners might call her a victim, but she wouldn't allow herself to be victimized, and that was a good lesson to remember. You had to give her respect as an *everywoman*; she was your mother, your sister, your wife, or your wild lover, not some Victorian maiden who considered sex an evil necessity. She was an inspiration, driven into situational sin but able to change her fate bravely—a woman you'd want to take a chance with if she'd have you.

Sometimes typecasting occurs unintentionally or when we romanticize the past. A century of writers created and then preserved stereotypes. Characterizations of prostitutes and madams as "harpies" or angels with a "heart of gold," and portrayals of the sex trade as merely a lucrative business opportunity are oversimplifications that impede genuine understanding. Surely some women got out with a fortune, but that was more an exception than the rule. More often than not, their choices were a matter of survival.

It's fascinating to look at the literature of the day. Great writers such as Bret Harte and Mark Twain helped fuel and shape the East Coast's fascination with the lawless West. They wrote of jumping frogs, outlaws, miners, gamblers, and the shady ladies in anarchic gold camps on the frontier. Newspapers, magazines, and pulp fiction followed suit, fanning the fascination and shaping our developing nation's cultural imagination. They exaggerated the violence, promoting showdowns, fast guns, outlaws, and hyperbolic exaltation—the cult of the cowboy. Life in the West was reduced to a high-contrast struggle between good and evil. In the lawless land, absent of structure, the base nature of men emerged. They needed the pure, the mild, the galvanizing influence of a true woman to tame their inner beast.

Prostitution was of particular interest. We read about the extremes in two stories by Bret Harte: "The Outcasts of Poker Flat" and "Luck of Roaring Camp." In "Poker Flat," we see the old fallen madam, Duchess, who has a heart of gold; she starves herself to death so there's more food for Piney, a fifteen-year-old who is eloping with her true love. Duchess' final sacrifice makes her look like a virgin in death. In "Roaring Camp," the only woman in town is a fallen whore named Cherokee Sal, who has corrupted the men's collective morality. She dies in childbirth. Her baby, Luck, helps change the men, who decide they have to alter their carnal ways so they can raise the boy properly.

In this milieu, Red Stockings' homage to duty, her reverence for her family's good name, would be respected. In a male-dominated community—like any mining camp—the men lived by a loose and eccentric code of honor. For example, Jack McCall—the man who shot Wild Bill Hickok in the back—was acquitted in a miner's court. McCall said Wild Bill had killed his brother. Putting a bullet in the gambling gunfighter was his way of evening the score; it was an act of honor, not murder. (McCall was later convicted in federal court and hanged for the murder.) These men lived reckless, dangerous, and irresponsible lives. They might work fifteen hours a day only to spend a summer's earnings on one wild night in town. In the morning, flat broke and hungover, they would start over. There was a live-and-let-live attitude, since the entertainment in town was generally centered on several of the seven deadly sins. A few got truly rich—enough to fan the dream of wealth. Most men ended up working for wages. In the first year, there were 400 working claims on California Gulch. An average claim could yield 130 to 140 ounces of gold a year. Today, that's just under $700 a day—good money, but not enough for everyone. Nor did it last. After the "low-hanging fruit" was plucked, it took money and know-how to scale a mine. The early years of Leadville weren't different from those of most mining towns. The town started as a collection of camps.

Miners were represented as big-hearted, warm, and friendly. They made money and spent it freely. Their morality might seem a little convoluted from our modern perspective, but it was uniquely frontier. It was less presumptuous, if not a tattered form of romanticism. Their world was dangerous, so they admired bravery and self-reliance. As one man said, "They'd give up all their gold for [a] night with a bawdy woman or give up their lives fighting for another woman's honor." A miner was willing to forgive a scarlet woman if she vowed never again to stray off the honorable path. Some certainly saw the irony of their lifestyles. Isolation made it easier to give absolution. They would've liked the strong-willed Hester Prynne in *The Scarlet Letter*, the woman who faced her punishment alone, not allowing it to destroy her spirit. They would've respected her for taking the blame.

Of course, historically such personalized models of honor aren't unique. Think of Southern duels, Western gunfights, knights in shining armor, Greek epics, or Disney and the cross-dressing heroine Mulan, a loyal daughter in a patriarchal society. She saves her family's honor by breaking taboo social boundaries. The Disney version ends happily, but other variations on the tale are imaginable if you're feeling a bit dark: she kills herself to remain a chaste warrior, gets married, becomes a prostitute, or all of the above.

The Red Stockings tale also benefits from timing. There's an air of mystery about her arrival in Leadville, but importantly, she was part of the town's creation myth. In a camp of men far from home, women were naturally scarce. A red-light woman held a level of respect that would dwindle as the town grew more settled. The living was rough, dangerous, and mostly devoid of social or cultural restraints. All the vices reigned wildly: drinking, gambling, vulgarity, and whoring (when available). There was a deferential attitude toward prostitutes, reflected in everyday speech that can be tracked in newspaper accounts. Kinder, euphemistic references were used, such as fallen angel, tender sister, fallen dove, soiled dove, sporting woman, or lady of the evening. As *Wall Street Journal* founder Charles H. Dow commented in a letter, reflecting on some of the Leadville working ladies, "[They are] attractive in appearance and are treated with all the respect that could be accorded to anybody."

If veins of ore ran deep, a mining camp was able to survive and grow. Naturally, attitudes shifted. The seven deadly sins became specialized. Big money—tens of millions of dollars—was made in Leadville. By 1879, according to the *Leadville Daily Chronicle*, there were 120 saloons, 19 beer halls, 115 gambling joints, and 35 bawdy houses. About 40 percent of the town's business interests were vice related, and of that number, 19 percent were technically illegal. As the town grew, respectability became important. In the Wild West, lascivious indulgences were part of a male-dominated culture. As the *wild* was taken out of the West, vices were segmented to certain districts on the wrong side of the tracks.

Before long, vices became subject to full-court moral presses. Reformers and women's movements started cleaning up their backyards. Drinking, gambling, and prostitution were the triple sins. By 1915, prostitution was illegal in Colorado; in 1916, the state legislature enacted Prohibition (four years before the national Volstead Act went into effect). Note the tone of this article about the red-light district in the *Herald Democrat* on August 14, 1891:

> *The vile language used and the drinking of beer and the smoking of cigarettes is not all, for they appear at the windows*

> *sometimes in the scantiest of clothing, bringing the blush of shame to the cheek of all respectable people who are unfortunate enough to see them. The conduct of these women has become so outrageous that respectable women are afraid to pass down that portion of Harrison avenue during the afternoon.*

For a time, Leadville would become the second-largest city in Colorado, a far cry from its austere beginnings. In the first few years, men spent winters in tents, searching for the mother lode. Cabins or shacks were poorly constructed and cold. The drinking water was contaminated by human waste. Imagine 10,000 gold-hungry men, all crammed together on steep hillsides. Garbage and refuse choked the streets. Unsanitary conditions spread diseases. Pneumonia was the biggest killer, followed by cholera, diphtheria, scarlet fever, typhoid, and smallpox. The elements took a horrific toll, too, along with avalanches and mining accidents. Suicide wasn't uncommon.

Winters were dreadful, long, and freezing. Exposure and the cumulative effects of continual cold were deadly. Malnutrition was a fact. Wood for heating and cooking fires, as well as cabins or shacks, became scarce. The forest seemed endless, but the resource was used up quickly. Even though the ground was often frozen, a miner would dig into what was called the *overburden*—the material above bedrock. He carried the overburden to a sluice box in a bucket or wheelbarrow. To make the sluice box, the miner felled trees and ripped boards with a handsaw. If a stream wasn't handy, he would build a ditch to re-channel the nearest water supply. The object was to collect the heavier gold dust, or better yet, chunks or nuggets, in the "riffs"—the parallel slats in the "troughs." These were made from two boards, eight to twelve feet long (using up more timber). The heavier material could then be re-sluiced or panned. If a place looked promising, shafts or tunnels would be dug. These would need to be shored up with yet again more timber.

So eager to find gold, many miners didn't build cabins or stockpile firewood for the long Colorado winter. Game was shot out quickly. What you didn't bring, you did without or bought at inflated prices. Before the railroad, everything had to be packed in on horses, mules,

A miner checks a sluice box for gold. PHOTOGRAPH BY HORACE S. POLEY (HORACE SWARTLEY), COURTESY OF DENVER PUBLIC LIBRARY, WESTERN HISTORY COLLECTION, P-1252.

or wagons, weather permitting. Many knew little about mining or surviving a ten-month winter at more than 10,000 feet above sea level. Mining is always dangerous, but ignorance made it more so.

We can't blame the Leadville miners—or the women on the line—for their hopes and dreams and for their celebration of a girl named Red Stockings. Such dreams are what make us human.

Here's another story. It's about Ruth Davenport, a working girl who got a few lines in a Colorado newspaper. She was pretty, vivacious, and full of life. Ruth had dreams and aspirations, too, but she wasn't as lucky as Red Stockings. They said the music in the dance hall stopped when she died—out of respect—but then life went on, without fanfare or a mythology to last 150 years. Her only eulogy came from the *Cripple Creek Times*, January 21, 1896:

> *On a bed in a dingy room lay a woman, an unfortunate woman. Around her stood other unfortunate women who shed tears and administered to the woman's wants as well as their untrained hands could do. The sick woman was young, only nineteen*

years old, and exceedingly handsome, but the dreaded disease of pneumonia had driven her to bed and was slowly but surely closing her lungs. ☙

BESSIE RIVERS

The Durango Lady of the Red-Light District

Bessie Rivers arrived in Durango, Colorado, in the 1880s and ran an expensive brothel on the fourth floor of the luxurious Strater Hotel. Conveniently located above the First National Bank, the floor was jokingly referred to as Monkey Hall, referring to the monkey business that went on there. When Marguerite Jackson Cantrell was a young girl, she remembered seeing Bessie and her ladies riding in an open carriage. In an interview with Colorado history author Duane A. Smith, Cantrell said, "I used to watch those girls. They were so lovely, and they had their big hats on, their umbrellas, and one or two of them would be smoking, which you would not do in those days."

Bessie was a large woman, well-dressed and honest, at least in the sense that she wouldn't rob a client. It didn't mean she wouldn't charge high prices. Bessie also boasted that she hired honest girls. She kept a large safe so she could secure valuables for customers who were otherwise occupied. The house was expensively furnished

A woman working in a bordello would keep her finery in a chest, often at the foot of her bed.
PHOTOGRAPH BY MICHAEL RUTTER.

with imported furniture. You could pay in gold, gold dust, silver, or cash. Some were allowed a line of credit. Bessie was a fixture in Durango. She made no pretense about what she did for a living; in fact, she advertised rather aggressively.

Sinner though she was, Bessie was well liked and considered a good businesswoman. She also enjoyed photography. The Durango Democrat *reported in 1908, "She is yet in the flesh trade, tender, confiding and adored." She was well connected and paid her fines, knowing a thing or two about influence peddling. But by 1911, she was growing tired of her trade and tried retirement.*

Is the Strater Hotel haunted? Even today, many people claim to have seen and heard spooky things, and such stories abound in the journals included in each guestroom. Reportedly, the spirit of a prostitute named "Swede" Anna Van Camp still haunts its halls. According to the Durango Democrat*, it took poor Anna several bloody tries to commit suicide. Apparently, she used a penknife to stab herself under the left breast—then stabbed herself several more times. She then slit her throat.*

3

Mattie Silks

The Denver Madam with an Accountant's Mind

HER BUSINESS PLAN WAS SIMPLE: "Men taken in and done for." In an interview before she died, Mattie said she went into the sporting life solely for business reasons—she considered herself a businesswoman. "I operated the best house in town, and I had, as my clients, the most important men in the West."

During the late 1880s and through the 1890s—her prime earning years—Mattie's yearly net worth was probably over $500,000 (by today's standards, that's about $13 million). She died with money in the bank. A woman making millions over the life of her career was a rarity in a business that was so transitory—especially when we realize that a skilled craftsman in the 1890s (a bricklayer, for example) could earn $3.25 a day (under $1,000 a year). A woman in a factory might earn $3 to $5 dollars a week (under $250 a year), while a schoolteacher would earn a little more.

Always a romantic, Mattie was kind, controlling, and hyperbolic. She admired Lillie Langtry and Queen Victoria, fashioning her stodgy wardrobe after the slightly bawdy socialite actress and the popular queen. Mattie lived the high life, with champagne, according to her personal maid, being her drink of choice.

She was accused of being iron-fisted, fiscally clever, but fair with her employees—all of which is true. Ironically, she was frequently blindsided by "sweet-talking" men who took her heart and her money. In affairs of the heart, she wasn't clever. One of these men, Cortez Thompson, beat the living hell out of her several times in drunken rages. When she was seventy-seven, after Cortez died, Mattie married a younger man. Always looking for a lasting, meaningful relationship, she was often disappointed. She tended to be attracted mostly to gamblers looking for a ride and a bankroll.

MATTIE BOUGHT PROPERTY, invested, and expanded her business interests. She owned a ranch, raised horses, lived in opulent houses, and traveled internationally. She said she learned how to shoot from Wild Bill Hickok in the early 1870s when she was a rookie madam in Abilene, Texas. (Of course, after he was dead, a lot of folks said they knew Wild Bill.) Fortunately, she was a poor pupil, missing those she aimed at with her infamous pearl-handled pistol. Nevertheless, Madam Silks was one of the few women who made the transition from the Old West into the twentieth century. She did business in the Klondike, and she knew how to keep municipal leaders happily bribed, saying it was easier to pay bribes and fines in advance to avoid raids and gain protection from the police force; $50 a day was a small price to pay.

Her real name was Martha Thompson, but everyone called her Mattie. We're not sure exactly when she was born—probably in 1847 or 1848—possibly in Fayette County, Pennsylvania. She was probably raised in Indiana. Mattie was always reticent about the details. She rarely talked about her childhood, but she hinted that she came from a hardworking but poor family. She liked clothes, fancy curtains, and delicate decorations and lace. She liked what money could buy.

She was an influential force to be reckoned with. She rose to prominence playing a complicated game of business chess that would have made the Medici merchants proud. Her business thrived for half a century. Prostitution, she stated, "was a way to make money." She was a famous woman in her day—and still is—but she was cloaked in folklore, some of which she surely fostered. Mattie, like her friend Jennie Rogers, produced some pithy sound bites. We have a lot of lore, but for a woman who did business for so long, we sadly *know* precious little. Census records and newspaper accounts help, but they're superficial. Mattie never talked about her personal life or how she felt. We get fascinating historical teasers and glimpses but have little else. So much of what we know is secondhand observation and newspaper accounts; there is a core of information, but it twists and leaves no clear picture. On the other hand, most of the prostitutes and madams who worked in Denver are today nameless.

Mattie spent ten years working and managing brothels in places like Springfield, Illinois, and Hays and Dodge City, Kansas. She also ran a freighting business of sorts—a so-called "Hell on Wheels" of itinerant prostitution, taking her girls and drinks to rail camps and boomtowns by covered wagon. On one trip, she brought a canvas bathtub. Amid the confusion of her trade, Mattie insisted, proudly, that she was a madam, but she also claimed that she never was a prostitute. This obviously is a stretch; translated from Mattie's lexicon, it means she was never arrested or officially charged. She was run out of Springfield "on a rail" during a moral purge, but this didn't seem to count in her mind.

In 1875, Mattie moved to Georgetown, Colorado, because she was tired of the vagaries of prairie towns and cowboys. She wanted a slice of the big money being made in the gold camps. There was gold dust—lots of gold dust—to be gleaned from lonely miners.

As a young entrepreneur in Georgetown, while running a successful bordello on Brownell Street named the Silver Queen of the Rockies, Mattie got sidetracked. The diversion was a card-playing gambler named George Silks. Most likely, they married in one fashion or another. They may have been the parents of a child; we don't know. Nevertheless, George was "cuckolded" by his lady, whom he discovered had a mind of her own. In spite of his shame, he followed her to Denver, then drifted out of her life, moving on to other boomtowns.

(Some tales suggest Mattie took on the name of Silks at an earlier point in her career because she liked silk dresses. This doesn't seem likely, but it's a good story.)

Her relationship with George Silks certainly wasn't long, and she didn't pretend to be a faithful wife. She had a public, if not dramatic, affair when she set her cap for Cortez "Cort" Thompson. He was a gambler, drifter, and accomplished foot racer. All sorts of races were taken seriously in frontier towns. Foot races, as well as horse races, drew crowds. One particular event at the fairgrounds was sponsored by volunteer firemen. It was a cause for celebration, drinking, and gambling. Cort, at long odds, won the 125-yard dash, handily beating veteran racer Sam Doherty. Mattie won $2,000 in gold dust. The story goes that she carried her earnings back to her parlor in a most unladylike fashion—in the lap of her skirt.

Thompson, the celebrated runner, and Mattie, the madam, became a topic of conversation. Cort was married, with a wife and child in another town. Newspaper accounts discussed some of his races, in which he was known as an opportunist. He was suspected of throwing an occasional race if it profited him. Obviously, some of the stories about him are true, but his myth grew in Mattie's larger shadow, and that sometimes bothered him. He was from Texas and bragged about riding with William Quantrill during the Civil War. He tried to be a bad man, a big shot, and is rumored to have worn two guns in fancy holsters. He wasn't much taller than Mattie, and while he was thin when they first met, easy living added some pounds. Some thought him good-looking. He had Southern manners and mostly enjoyed the good life. He preferred gambling to working and liked fancy clothes. He was a philanderer and drinker. Frankly, Cortez D. Thompson was Mattie's expensive kept man, a spoiled toy. For the woman who seemed to have everything, she indulged and doted on him at great personal and emotional expense. In addition to the cost of keeping such a man, she covered his gambling debts, which experts suggest could have been—in today's dollars—millions.

She took 40 to 50 percent of what her "boarders" earned. She provided them with nice rooms and laundry service. Her women were expected to be polite and dress well. A large portion of her women's income was spent on clothing, which Mattie certainly profited from. In her houses, there were maids and servants and more protection than one would have in a common brothel. Mattie kept records of the men who visited her establishment, and if one proved "ungentlemanly," he wouldn't be allowed to return. She often greeted her callers at the door personally and brought them into the drawing room. There would be music and offerings of fine food and drink, among other menus. Liquor sales were lucrative.

Mattie was likable and lived in a down-home way; she wasn't known for the sophisticated grace, elegance, and poise that came more naturally to Jennie Rogers and Ella Wellington. She admired her colleagues' tastes in clothes and tried to follow the latest trends, but she always looked stodgy. For example, the custom *de Medici* frock she often wore seemed a bit pathetic, almost comical. Even some of her peers thought her costume choices were tasteless, although they wouldn't say it to her face. As she got older, her clothing got more expensive and out of tune. Laura Evens, who liked Mattie, privately said she dressed like an old whore.

Mattie's fashion tastes were unusual even for the times. PHOTOGRAPH DONATED TO THE DENVER PUBLIC LIBRARY BY *ROCKY MOUNTAIN NEWS*, RMN-046-9218.

In 1875 or 1876, while in her late twenties, Mattie moved to Denver with money in her purse. Business had been good. She'd left Georgetown in search of even bigger profits. She reportedly paid $13,000, which was quite a sum, to Nell French for a nice, working brothel and didn't look back. The building was three stories tall and had plenty of room.

Mattie believed in God and always wore a

diamond-studded cross around her neck, but she wasn't a plaster saint and would do whatever she could to get what she wanted. As she grew older, Mattie seemed to espouse propriety and servility, but she had a temper. Running her business carefully, she didn't put up with women who violated her rules or tried to steal her man. She said, "I never took a girl into my house who had had no previous experience of life and men. This was a rule of mine. No innocent young girl was hired." In 1877, the newspaper reported that Mattie was fined for public intoxication. Later, the *Rocky Mountain News* carried stories about an angry Mattie punching one Katie Fulton in the head and knocking her down. When Katie tried to get up, Mattie kicked her in the face (some articles say this broke her nose). Apparently, that wasn't enough, since Katie had been or was trying to be overly familiar with Thompson. Tales say that Mattie took a shot at her from a carriage but missed.

In 1884, Mattie learned that Thompson's wife had died and they were free to marry. A tempestuous, seven-year engagement could finally be solemnized. On July 5, they were joined in matrimony by the Reverend Daniel. Cort wasn't really interested in his daughter, Rita, from his former wife. He'd never seen Rita and wasn't anxious to be responsible for the child. Apparently, Cort would have let Rita live as an orphan. He also said he didn't want the girl brought up in a whorehouse. Mattie, anxious for an instant family so she could play house, affectionately supported the girl in a boarding school.

By all accounts, Mattie had a good relationship with her adopted daughter. She told Cort to buy a place where they could meet on neutral ground. The couple started a ranch near Wray, Colorado, about 170 miles east of Denver. Foolishly, Mattie let Cort purchase it in his name. (He was a gold digger, and she was indulging him like a lapdog. She'd later have to call in favors to get the deed back from Cort.) She enjoyed ranch life and secretly thought an outdoor lifestyle might keep her husband from drinking and chasing other women. Mattie bought a horse named Jim Blaine, which made money on the racing circuit. She also acquired other horses to build a bloodline.

One of the most famous Mattie Silks tales occurred in the 1880s. She claimed that she did her best to bring more rail traffic to the Mile

High City. Because several city officials hoped to gain advantage, Mattie—always eager to curry favor—used her special professional skills when called upon. Apparently, an important decision-maker from the East Coast, someone who could swing a deal, had a special interest in the good madam. He wanted Mattie to join him on a month-long vacation in his private rail coach as he went to the West Coast on business. The Denver businessmen had a lot to gain. It just so happened that Mattie had a $5,000 note due and was nervous about leaving. She was also likely nervous about Cort's extracurricular activities. The chamber of commerce was persuasive and agreed to pay her note if she would help "persuade" the East Coast businessman with her many charms. So with Thompson's blessing and a promise to be good, she went. She traveled in the man's exclusive, private coach. She even extended her visit; apparently she was so congenial that he wanted her companionship for another thirty days as the two also visited the East Coast. He even introduced her as his wife. She loved to talk about how she mingled with ease among the rich and famous. In the end, the Denver businessmen paid her note, but she failed to get the deal.

Mattie was dramatic and made good copy, and good copy was good business. She was also fiery and temperamental. On March 13, 1891, at the Lucky Chance Saloon (or so the story goes), a tear-streaked, angry Mattie burst in, ready to catch her lover being unfaithful. The infamous madam made a spectacle of herself, ignominiously rushing past drunks and gamblers and pushing up the stairs. They knew why she was there. Pearl-handled pistol in hand, Mattie went into the third room, said something, and took a few shots at a naked woman. Presumably Cort knew his wife's moods and quickly got out of the way. One of the bullets is said to have clipped a henna-colored lock from the head of a woman named Lillie Dab before she rolled off the bed, unhurt. Lore says that Cort coldcocked Mattie with the butt of his Colt. Another version has him wrestling the pearl-handled pistol from Mattie, who then hit him over the head. He beat her in his rage. Embarrassed by the black and blue blemishes from the beating, she filed for divorce. Her "true love" had been sidetracked by Lillie Dab. Apparently he'd tried to transfer some of their marital assets to Lillie, including the horse ranch. By a court order, he was blocked from selling the ranch and other assets. Mattie had powerful friends in public office and was a financial powerhouse in her own right. Even in a man's world, Thompson didn't stand a chance. This time, his half-a-million-dollar meal ticket was about to walk away, and then where would he be? He promised to control his wandering eye and never to see the henna-haired tart again. He also agreed to transfer the title of the ranch to Mattie. They kissed and made up. In less than two weeks, she dropped the divorce proceedings.

The story repeated: he wandered and drank, they fought, and he was physically abusive. One time, she went with him to Kansas City to rest and visit the racetrack at Overland Park. She became interested in horse racing and bought a ranch in Yuma County, Colorado, for Cort to manage. They fought again and again. She threatened to leave him. He promised to behave, and she took him back and treated him to tailored clothes, fine wine, and money to gamble with. He'd always been a poor gambler and lost a lot of her money. He said he felt like one of her pets, and rightly so, but he liked the lifestyle she provided and didn't have enough courage to try to live on his own. He also liked owning a horse ranch.

Mattie (left) enjoyed owning fine horses, including this one trained by Frank Nott, a livery stable owner who, like Mattie, had moved from Georgetown to Denver. PHOTOGRAPH COURTESY OF DENVER PUBLIC LIBRARY WESTERN HISTORY COLLECTION, DPL X-27055.

On June 27, 1897, Mattie—the reigning queen of Denver's red-light district for twenty years—went to pay her respects to Queen Victoria of England. Mattie was an avowed Anglophile, and she took her husband along to attend the queen's diamond jubilee, along with over a million well-wishers. The pair lived in grand style. While in England, Cort bought his wife an expensive mink coat, which Mattie proudly wore to horse races back in Colorado.

Business back home had slowed. A string of Jack-the-Ripper-style murders in Denver took a toll on the Tenderloin District. Mattie put bars on her windows. She also could sense a change in public opinion as Denver settled down. Smelling profit in the well-publicized Klondike, Mattie was ready for a new adventure up north. Following the business model she'd used in her first decade of business, she would go to the goldfields with sporting women. Selecting eight of her beauties to accompany her, she and Cort set out in the winter of 1898. It was cold, and the journey itself was adventurous, with a fair share of peril. They traveled over frozen paths to the newest gold country. Originally, Mattie thought she might work in Skagway, perhaps for the infamous Soapy Smith, but she changed her mind. Distrusting Smith, she followed her hunch, feeling that she'd make more if she went farther north. Mattie was eager for a new frontier, but the trip north proved difficult. The fact that she could sell whiskey and champagne for $130 a gallon was a pleasing thought.

Mattie rented a building in Dawson City, Yukon, and set up shop. She paid $350 a month for rent. She also paid $1,500 a month to the Royal Canadian Mounted Police for protection and bribes. Prostitution was illegal in Canada, but Inspector Charles Constantine and his men looked the other way. The inspector did have standards, however. He blinked at working women, but he outlawed women wearing pants or bloomers, which he considered disgraceful and immoral. Also, the word *prostitute* was banned from publications; euphemisms were insisted upon.

Mattie did a whopping business, while her husband played faro. He spent most of his time in Joe Cooper's Dominion Saloon, losing money. Mattie was competing with Madam Beatrice Larnne and the famous Madam "Diamond Lil" Davenport via Skagway (the beautiful but hardened woman from the wrong side of the tracks in Chicago;

she was a stunning, six-foot-tall woman who enjoyed scandalous dime novels). Each of the madams got quite rich.

Doing business in the north, however, was expensive. The summer was wet and cool, and Mattie worried about her husband's health; he had a cold that he couldn't shake. She didn't want to face a northern winter again. After paying off her husband's gambling debts, Mattie cleared around $40,000 in about five months, even factoring in the cost of the trip. Then they returned to the lower forty-eight.

The dry weather seemed to help Cort recover. He wanted to buy cattle for the ranch. Mattie thought 5,000 head was too much—she was still stinging from how much she'd had to pay to clear his debt in the Yukon. She gave him $1,500. He headed to the couple's ranch but spent the money on drinks and threatened to sell her racehorse, Jim Blaine. She phoned the Yuma County sheriff and told him to arrest her husband until she arrived.

When she arrived, she found her husband quite ill. He said he'd been poisoned by bad oysters. The doctor said there was little he could do. Jack was diagnosed with ptomaine poisoning (likely aggravated by his alcoholism). The physician prescribed a mixture of whiskey and laudanum. The couple's last exchanges were typically dramatic. Cort blamed his wife for trying to poison him and said that if he had a gun, he'd shoot her. Legend has it that Mattie pulled out the pistol she carried and handed it to him, saying something like, "If you are going to die, I want to die." Cort died on April 12, 1900, leaving a grief-stricken Mattie. She sent him to his reward with an expensive funeral. He was buried in Fairmount Cemetery in Denver.

After Cort's death, Mattie understood that her world had changed. Most of her friends were gone, and she was getting old and tired. She tried other ventures, one of which was the Silks Hotel, and in 1911 she bought Jennie Rogers' House of Mirrors and installed her own name in tile in the entryway. She visited the child she had adopted. Later, she hired a bookkeeper named Jack Ready, sometimes called Handsome Jack. They married. The vice laws had changed, and so had the open tolerance of prostitution.

In 1924, Mattie closed the House of Mirrors and her other properties. She broke her hip at a party in December 1928 and died in

Denver Hospital on January 7, 1929. She had a Quaker funeral service and was buried next to Cort. Her grave marker read Martha A. Ready. She'd lived a lavish life and managed to spend most of the money she earned. She left Handsome Jack about $4,000, her studded cross necklace, and a few other pieces of jewelry. He thought it would be more. He died a few years later—penniless—and was placed in an unmarked grave.

MINNIE SMITH

Mean-Tempered Madam Who Whipped a Man Cheating at Cards

Also known as Lou Eaton and "Dirty Alice," Minnie was reportedly a skinny, ill-tempered madam with a serious addiction to gambling. She was not considered attractive by any standard, but her quarrelsome personality didn't help either. According to the mythology surrounding her, the misanthropic madam clubbed a lawyer to death with the butt of her revolver. Mean Minnie was not above abusing one of her girls or a client.

She worked in Denver and Buena Vista and owned parlor houses in Creede and Cripple Creek. She did a lot of business in Colorado City. She had a checkered career, and few seemed sad to see her leave town. Once, she was recruiting ladies in Denver and got drunk and disorderly. The police threw her in jail. She promised to pay her fine and they let her out, but she skipped town. The police were likely relieved.

Minnie is said to have taken a riding whip to a man who tried to cheat her at cards. "I hate a cheat," she said. Magazines of her day lampooned her temper tantrums and showed woodcuts or cartoons of her whipping men. She had so many confrontations with the law that it was hard to track them all. She was known for her violent outbursts, which apparently did not scare off her clients.

In her early years, Minnie was quite a gambler. She made money, but by the time she was in her forties, alcohol and opium were taking their toll. Her fits of melancholy grew longer. In 1893, life was too much. She overdosed on morphine and never woke up. According to the Colorado Daily Chieftain, *Minnie was buried next to her first husband, Royster Smith, in Evergreen Cemetery in Colorado Springs.*

4

Jennie Rogers

"I Shot Him Because I Love Him! Damn Him!"

JENNIE ROGERS WAS A COMMANDING WOMAN—six feet tall with dark black hair. She wore velvet dresses and emerald earrings. Living well was important to her. She liked to get her way, and she played to win. One day, she surprised her young lover in Salt Lake City, but the surprise was on her.

"I shot him because I love him! Damn him!" she said when the Salt Lake City police arrived. She was arrested and put in jail for attempted murder.

Fortunately, Jennie was a better businesswoman than a pistol shot. She invested, speculated in real estate, and built the notorious House of Mirrors on Denver's Holladay Street. She ruled her world as if it were a fiefdom and wasn't above underhanded dealings. With the help of a Midwestern policeman, she and her group of investors blackmailed a Denver businessman into bankrolling her largest venture. She ran her business like a Wharton MBA. However, her personal life was another matter. She often acted like an impulsive teenager. Her husbands and lovers cost her several fortunes.

JENNIE HAD AN EYE FOR FASHION, but she was comfortable among working men—as long as they had money. She sweated the details and often orchestrated what her parlor ladies wore. Unlike her friend and competitor Mattie Silks, who was said to be a mule with a fancy and expensive saddle, Jennie could behave like a thoroughbred. She had an intuitive feel for image and branding and took a cut from the dressmakers and fabric merchants for her time. She knew how to use people to accomplish her purposes. Like Scarlett O'Hara in *Gone with the Wind*, Jennie wasn't going to be poor again and was willing to do whatever she needed to maintain her lifestyle.

She liked attending the opera, wearing expensive clothes, and drinking imported liquor. The lady had a soft spot in her heart for animals, especially dogs and horses. It would have surprised many of her patrons to know that years earlier she had worked in the fields like a common laborer—a pretty girl with a frequently washed dress and dirty fingernails. She never forgot the humiliation she felt hocking vegetables in the streets of Pittsburgh to get enough money to help feed her family.

Jennie Rogers was her professional name, but she was known by other names, including Leeah J. Tehume and Leah J. Fries (the name she used on many of her Colorado property deeds). She was born Leeah Calvington on July 4, 1843, in Alleghany, Pennsylvania, into poverty. We don't know much about her family or her relationship with them. Her father had a hard time keeping food on the table. As a girl, Jennie helped all she could. When she got a little older, she would go into the city to sell produce.

A tall, beautiful girl, she noticed that when she flirted with men and boys, she sold more produce. She disliked the rigors of farm life and wished she had enough money to buy new clothes and stay at nice places. Jennie was a spirited young woman who had plans, and they didn't include a two-bit dirt farm in Pennsylvania. A comely girl bursting out of her clothes, she entertained a number of marriage proposals. Her parents were also eager for her to have a more comfortable life, a life that might shower some of the good things of the world back on them. Some histories suggest that she was educated, but her associate and fellow madam, Laura Evens, opined that Jennie was not literate.

Her family thought it fortuitous when Dr. G. Friess asked for her hand in marriage. As a doctor's wife, she had a life of ease.

However, for a girl eager for bright lights, being the young wife of a busy, older doctor was not what she'd imagined. She did have the physical comforts she'd only rarely enjoyed before, as well as few responsibilities, but she grew bored. She ran off with a steamboat captain by the name of Rogers, a pilot on the Missouri River. Being on a boat and seeing new places must have been exciting, but after two years the small cabin and muddy waterway got tedious, so she again ran away.

Jennie found work as a housekeeper for a city mayor, but her free spirit again got the better of her. Apparently, in a casual moment, she mentioned unapologetically that she had left two men. For a respectable household, this was too much. She either quit or was fired. The mayor couldn't afford any political fallout. The rumor of a trampy domestic would've been bad for his image.

Jennie re-created herself with a new professional persona. The details are obscure and so is the timeline, but she was able to open a brothel in St. Louis. She thought that being a madam would give her the means she needed and the control over her life she craved. Wanting to expand—or perhaps she had to leave St. Louis because of a scandal—she heard about Denver and took a trip to see if there was opportunity for her there. She also considered relocating to California. Denver suited her, so in January 1880 she bought a property for $4,600 in cash on "wicked" Holladay Street, the hub of the city's red-light district. She bought it from none other than Mattie Silks, who would become her good friend and business rival. This wasn't unusual—madams often bought and sold property among their peers. In March of that same year, newspaper reports suggested that Jennie was arrested for "unladylike conduct." Legend has it that she was fined for racing horses in the street, taking drugs, being a vagrant, and running a disorderly house. She was riding the fringe of a moral scourge, so the police were especially vigilant and public about arrests.

When anyone writes about prostitution in Denver, Holladay Street is nearly always mentioned. It's confusing because Holladay is also referred to as Market Street—the names are interchanged. Here's why: Holladay was named after Denver pioneer Ben Holladay. It was renamed Market Street in 1889. The Holladay family was embarrassed and thought their family name was being tarred by brothels, gambling joints, and saloons. Thus, the "bawdiest," the "wickedest," street in Denver got a name makeover. Some newspapers, magazines, and historical accounts assume readers know the history and use Holladay and Market Street interchangeably, sometimes in the same paragraph.

Jennie set up business on "the row" on Holladay Street. Tales grew tall quickly. Intrigue followed her, painting her as mysterious and enticing, a checkbox for lonely men with a lot of money. Myth has Jennie making back her investment in a month, which seems optimistic, even for a venal city like post–Civil War Denver, but it's possible. She saw opportunity, sold her Midwestern interests, and made the Mile High City her home. She expanded and opened up other opulent parlors, including her dream brothel: the infamously decadent House of Mirrors, which had twenty-seven rooms—including sixteen bedrooms—and a bathroom.

We know some of what she thought from secondhand observation and infrequent statements and accounts in newspapers. Little is known about what she felt about her day-to-day life or her philosophy. What we have is a catalogue of Jennie lore, which includes many interesting stories and variations of the same story.

Perhaps with the urging of her current lover or possibly a group of important clients, Jennie helped blackmail "some" or "one" of her patrons. Undoubtedly, she was interested in the money, but she likely was also concerned with maintaining her influence among the local power brokers. At their urging—or perhaps hers—she gathered incriminating evidence on a man or men who didn't want his family, or their families, to know about after-hours activities. The con was to try to get him, or them, to pay a hefty sum to keep dirty secrets from going public.

Jennie had a lover-friend-client who was an official in the police department back in St. Louis. They'd stayed in contact. Supposedly he made visits to Denver so they could, ahem, renew their friendship. One of Denver's prominent citizens had a former wife who had run off or died. He'd since remarried into a wealthy family and didn't want a scandal to embarrass his wealthy new in-laws, impede his deals, or cause social embarrassment. Someone—Jennie—started talking

Rogers' House of Mirrors was elegant in its day, with floor-to-ceiling mirrors in the front reception room, crystal chandeliers, a grand piano, and intricate carvings on its façade. PHOTOGRAPH COURTESY OF THE FRED M. MAZZULLA COLLECTION, HISTORY COLORADO.

about how he might have murdered his first wife. Here the story takes a number of interesting twists. The St. Louis policeman is said to have found an old skull, perhaps that of an Indian, and buried it in the man's backyard. Later, in some official or semi-official capacity, the out-of-town officer showed up to investigate. The Denver man was likely innocent but didn't want the notoriety. Apparently, Jennie also told the poor sap she had more proof that he had killed his first wife and would give the evidence to the chief of police. The man relented and gave Jennie thousands of dollars.

Jennie built the House of Mirrors with her illicit funds. In 1888, she leased a house at 512 Holladay Street from Minnie Clifford, with the agreement that she would buy it. They must have had a falling out, because Minnie sold the property to someone else for a good profit. Jennie angrily went to the buyer with an even better offer and bought it back.

The House of Mirrors was extremely expensive and laden with overruns. Jennie often hosted important men and knew more than she should about their personal and business matters. Her new place would become a second home for local government officials. She had silent investors who were willing to support her ventures, not only because she had proven to be a good investment, but also to keep their secrets from seeing the light of day. She wasn't above subtle bribery and extortion to get what she wanted. She cultivated important men as one might cultivate a garden's prize-winning roses. Apparently, her girls provided company for the Denver chief of police and his cronies. Some folklore suggests that she might have been the chief's lover. The chief was her instant connection to law enforcement if a bribe to cover some illegal activity didn't pan out. He also shielded her from raids and personally collected her fines.

Her stock-in-trade was to have the best of everything and then charge extra for clients to enjoy it. She hired William Quayle, the noted architect, to remodel her house with all the extras: three stories with fancy rooms, a wine cellar, servants' quarters, a large dining room, a spacious kitchen, a ballroom, and bedrooms. There were mirrors on the ceilings and walls, crystal chandeliers, and imported rugs. Her house was so lavish that local businessmen and politicians held meetings there. A chagrined *Rocky Mountain News* reporter wrote in 1890, "Each afternoon about three o'clock, the august lawmakers would retire to Jennie Rogers' Palace of Joy on Market Street and there deport themselves in riotous fashion."

Along with Mattie Silks, Jennie was one of the two reigning "queens of Denver's Red Light Row." But as the Iron Madam who battled her way to financial security, she had an Achilles' heel. It was all too predictable: she was at the top of the business game, but it wasn't enough. She was lonely and wanted to share her life with someone who loved her. For a woman who made her living reading men and playing elaborate parlor-house games of love, she was vulnerable. Similar to Mattie Silks and Ella Wellington, all alumni owners of the House of Mirrors, Jennie tried to groom younger men to be her special, ideal love interests. In a profession that was deceptive and shadowy by nature—and having been deceitful and unfaithful herself—she nevertheless wanted to have a fulfilling relationship. She got blindsided and misled. One evening, she noticed a carriage driver who was especially good to his horses. His name was John A. Wood, but he went by Jack. As a fellow horse lover, he drew her attention. They struck up a conversation and hit it off. Jack, she discovered, was also a bartender.

It was a fairy-tale romance that, for a while, seemed like magic. Jennie Rogers, the madam, and the young coachman and bartender were like star-crossed lovers. We don't know if he was an unwitting provocateur or an opportunist, but they became a public item. Perhaps because she didn't meet him professionally, he caught her off guard. Jack seemed like a good man: handsome, quietly refined. She fell like a bowling pin. In spite of the difference in their ages (Jennie was older by a good measure), some have suggested that they were like a couple of children at a circus.

She bought a small saloon in Salt Lake City and set Jack up in business. It was a good investment. She thought Jack could better himself, and he proved to be a good manager. It was perfect because she could keep her business life removed from her personal life. She made frequent visits to Salt Lake City so they could be together.

Jennie was happy to have someone who really loved her, someone who wasn't after her money. So on a whim one day, she bought a train ticket to visit her true love, Jack. She burst into their love nest unannounced, the love nest that *she* had bought for the two of them. It didn't turn out the way she'd planned. The surprise was on her. She found her lover in a compromising position with a younger woman. Jennie shouted and was angry and surprised and hurt all at the same time. Her heart was broken, and there was only one thing to do: kill him. Her famous temper flared, and she reached into her pocket and pulled out the trusty handgun she always carried. She pointed and fired—trying to blow away the only man she ever loved.

This incident seems like so many other madam-lover infidelity stories we've studied. Call it cliché or epic formula, it's a beloved part of the Western madam lore. The next part of the story might be familiar, too. In madam mythology, their aim doesn't seem to be good. As Jennie shot, the frightened Jack pushed the girl and tumbled over, but not before catching a bullet (only a flesh wound, a scratch). Jennie wondered if she had killed him. We assume the girl Jack had been with wisely ran off dressed in a sheet or a pillowcase—or something. The police quickly arrived, and Jennie uttered those famous lines, the words scorned madams are required to say at a time like this: "I shot him because I love him! Damn him!"

Jennie's famous temper had gotten the better of her. She was arrested and put in jail for attempted murder. Jack wasn't severely wounded and told police that the incident was his fault. Jennie was released, and she returned to Denver.

But Jack was not just another man. She didn't get over her two-timing lover and was depressed. She secretly hoped for a reconciliation. She was like a schoolgirl, unable to get over her first crush. She was wildly rich, but money hadn't made her happy. She kept tabs on Jack and after a few years swallowed her madam pride and wrote him a letter, telling him how she felt and how much she missed him. Jack was running a bar in Nebraska at the time, and to her delight—her added wealth surely didn't play a part—he wrote back. They became pen pals. And, to make the fairy tale more complete, the two reunited in 1889 and married on August 13. Tragically, a few years later, at age thirty-eight, Jack died suddenly. Again heartbroken, Jennie inscribed "He Is Not Dead, He Is Sleeping" on his headstone. To try to overcome her grief, she dove into her business concerns.

By the 1890s, Jennie's business ventures were doing well, but she was feeling worn down and tired. Her doctor diagnosed her with Bright's disease (an ailment of the kidneys that causes back pain, swelling, hypertension, and stomach problems). He told her that she needed to leave Denver and go to a lower altitude. Jennie was stubborn and reluctant to leave.

She sold the House of Mirrors. With the profits from her business, Jennie invested in real estate, water shares, and other opportunities. While Denver's vice proprietors managed to stay free of most legal entanglements, there were occasional officials who didn't share the "liberal" view of how city government should run. There were also outside influences, such as various women's movements, that demanded something be done about the corruption. To capitulate to these special-interest groups, city government now and then shook up the vice districts with showy arrests and added fines, but little changed overall. On one occasion, fifteen madams were arrested and fined for running disorderly houses, but all went back to work as soon as the officials pandered to the press to show how much they were doing to clean up the city. In 1892, Jennie, the most prominent madam of Denver, produced what was called the Red Book. It was a published catalogue for local vice, including the addresses and ads for places of gambling, drinking, and prostitution.

Jennie Rogers' fashion instincts ensured that she looked every bit the successful businesswoman. PHOTOGRAPH COURTESY OF HISTORY COLORADO.

This was her life, but it was wearing on her. She could tell that the times and attitudes were changing—the old days were quickly passing. Currying political favor only went so far. Prolonging her departure until she was quite sick, Jennie hired a manager for her business concerns and finally moved to Chicago. In the Windy City, she purchased another brothel after selling some of her assets. Jennie needed something, or someone, to keep her busy.

Archibald T. Thompson seemed just the man. He was a bit dumpy and gone to seed. He was balding and had great affection for her money. He made promises to her and promptly broke them. But a desperate Jennie stayed with him. She learned that he had other wives, but he promised that she was the only woman for him, and she believed him, while he kept spending her money. He bought her a ring—with her money—and took her on an expensive trip to the hot springs in Arkansas. Then, at age sixty-six on October 17, 1909, Jennie died, nearly broke, and was buried next to her beloved Jack. ൟ

5

'Poker' Alice Ivers

"Praise the Lord and Place Your Bets. I'll Take Your Money with No Regrets."

ALICE IVERS PLAYED A MAN'S GAME in a man's world. A paladin of cards, she was called Poker Alice. A sometime madam and lifelong Catholic, she insisted that her whores gather on the Sabbath so she could conduct Sunday school classes. In her long career, she was a bootlegger, a three-time widow, a mother to seven children, and a killer. No one questioned her skill with a deck of cards.

While poker, faro, and twenty-one were called games of chance, Alice understood that they were also games of skill—skill at cards as well as skill at reading people. When she was young and beautiful, men came to do battle on the green felt—a gaming table—like five-card knights honing their skills against an unlikely master who smoked cigars. She drew a crowd as handily as she drew an ace.

It wasn't considered dishonorable to lose to such a woman, unless your name was Jack "Lucky" Hardesty. He openly refused to play a man's game with a frill of a woman who didn't know her place. He said she'd cry if he took her money. He threw down the proverbial glove, and she picked it up and called his bluff.

"LUCKY" HARDESTY HAD TO LEARN THE HARD WAY. Perky Alice wasn't about to let him off easy. Like Hector and Achilles in an epic struggle, they battled one evening at the card table. Taking quick breaks to eat a sandwich or get a drink, they played relentlessly. By the end of the night, Alice had won $1,500 dollars. One onlooker said, "He lost like he had a hole in his pocket."

Saloon culture in the West reflected a man's world. Saloons might have been seen as an escape from the cares of the world, hard work, and domestic responsibility. At the least, they were a place for men to socialize. There was drinking, of course, and possibly fighting, whoring, and gambling, depending on the watering hole. This world was decidedly masculine. It was rarely a place for a woman, unless the woman was part of the furnishings. It wasn't that genteel and cultured refinements weren't important; they were. But so was the double standard (or at least the notion) that men needed their own space to be men.

Alice got her name honestly; she loved to gamble and was good at it. Lady gamblers were usually a draw for the house, mostly as fixtures or distractions. They would encourage men and create an atmosphere of daring and risk. They were someone for the men to show off to. Sometimes they were girls for hire or dancing partners.

Alice, however, wasn't a fixture. She was a draw for the house, but she was much more than a pretty dress; she was a player. Men wanted to best her. She had a head for cards and reading people. This sort of behavior for a "decent" woman was socially unacceptable. Nevertheless, men would come to watch her play, like you'd watch an athletic event or a chess game. In her heyday, she was said to be brilliant. A game of poker with her was playing against a legend.

Most of the images we have of Poker Alice are misleading: a weathered, heavy-set old woman—a hag in men's clothes—sporting a big cigar. It'd be easy to forget that in her youth she was an extraordinarily beautiful woman. These photographs were taken near the end of her long life. Those who knew her in her prime said she had a twinkle in her eyes that enchanted men and made them wistful. She would make more money in a week than a skilled craftsman could in months. After winning some big games, she would take the train to

New York for a luxurious vacation, sometimes buying a whole new wardrobe. She knew she was a good-looking woman. Nice clothes not only made her feel good, they were also tools of her trade. She dressed fashionably because men liked to gamble with a pretty woman. It was said she lowered her neckline to keep her opponents interested and distracted by her ample cleavage.

Like most gamblers, Alice moved from boomtown to boomtown, building a reputation that would follow her for the rest of her life. At one establishment, she reportedly broke the house. At some point, she picked up the unladylike habit of smoking cigars, which became one of her trademarks. She also developed another habit: drinking too much. This would catch up with her.

In her younger years, Alice was comely, equally capable of charming men and assessing their weaknesses.
PHOTOGRAPH COURTESY OF LEGENDS OF AMERICA.

Although she was educated, she couldn't see herself teaching school or sewing shirts for pennies an hour. Games of chance and the lifestyle they provided had gotten into her blood. She felt an excitement playing cards and loved everything about it. She'd say, "Praise the Lord and place your bets. I'll take your money with no regrets." According to folklore, she never worked on Sunday because she needed a day of rest, being a religious woman in her own way. She liked winning and taking a man's money fair and square. It was a lot easier than working for a living.

Alice claimed that she was born on February 17, 1853 (some sources say 1851), in England. This isn't certain, however; she might have been born in Virginia. We do know that her father, an Irishman named Ivers, was educated and saw to it that his children were, too. He was most likely a teacher, and the family did live in Virginia and later relocated to Colorado. Alice was good in school. It's not surprising that mathematics was her best subject. The attractive young woman turned the heads of the local boys, but she fell for a Leadville mining engineer named Frank Duffield, whom she married. Their union seemed happy, but it wouldn't last long.

The couple moved to Lake City, Colorado. On winter nights and during their free time, they played cards. Frank was a gambling enthusiast who taught his clever young wife how to play. Alice was a natural and soon bested her husband. Lore has it that Frank took her to card games, where she honed her craft. However, one fateful day, Frank miscalculated when he was setting off a charge of TNT in a mine shaft and blew himself into a thousand pieces. (Mining was and is a dangerous occupation.) Alice grieved, but at some point the pretty young widow had to make her way in the world. She could have taught school, but the pay was low and the hours long. The siren call from the cards was too loud to ignore.

For the most part, the reputation of a lady gambler—along with dance-hall women, hurdy-gurdy girls, actresses, and barmaids—was likely to be tainted by a scandalous whisper of prostitution. We don't know how her family reacted to her career choice, but her star was born. Perhaps her husband had also taught her how to shoot, or perhaps she learned it on the job. Regardless, she was known for being armed and handy with the gun she always carried. She caroused with a tough crowd, and carrying cash was an occupational requirement.

Through the 1880s, Alice worked the gambling circuit and cashed in on those who wanted to take her down a peg or two. By Alice's own account, she played poker in Leadville, Central City, Georgetown, Silver Plume, Creede, and other boomtowns. Sometimes her job description might be to watch over some of the soiled doves, which was considered women's work. Frequenting saloons and gambling halls, she understood and could manage prostitutes, but we don't have evidence that she was anything more than a gambler. There were rumors and legends, but most weren't true. For example, she never played cards with Wild Bill Hickok. She may have said, "Poor Wild Bill," when she heard he was murdered, but the two never met.

Gambling halls like this Leadville saloon, circa 1880s, were Alice's natural environment. PHOTOGRAPH COURTESY DENVER PUBLIC LIBRARY WESTERN HISTORY COLLECTION, X-6363.

Alice plied her trade in lively mining towns across Colorado, including Central City, shown here circa 1880. PHOTOGRAPH BY HARRY H. LAKE, COURTESY OF DENVER PUBLIC LIBRARY WESTERN HISTORY COLLECTION, L-613.

A man named Warren G. Tubbs was infatuated by the lovely lady and gracefully lost a few hands to her. Warren was a zealous gambler, but he wasn't really that good—or lucky—with cards. His day job was painting houses, and he dealt cards part-time. He was a better painter than card player, but he understood Alice. Over tables, the two got acquainted and eventually developed a romance—after Alice saved his life.

The story is told and retold of the good-natured Warren concentrating on his cards and not what was going on around him in the saloon. A drunken man came up behind him with a knife. Maybe Warren had beat him in a card game—we're not sure—but the man intended to get back his money or get even. Alice is said to have shot him handily. Such a thoughtful act grew into fondness and affection and then romance. The newly wedded lovebirds traveled, gambled, and settled into a routine. Alice was paid twenty-five dollars a night to play cards because her name drew customers. The couple bought a ranch and settled down. It was supposedly a happy match for decades, and neither gave up their gambling passion. Alice is said to have supplemented her "egg money" with poker winnings. They raised their children, with Alice apparently sliding off to make a few bucks and get out of the house for an evening or two a week. Whether she smoked around her children, we don't know. But the couple did their best to keep their children away from gambling and saloons. After the turn of the century, Warren died of either tuberculosis or pneumonia.

In her fifties, Alice opened the Poker Palace and brothel in Sturgis, South Dakota, and married a man named George Huckert. In the lore surrounding Alice, she either borrowed money from Huckert or owed him wages. In an interview, she commented that it was cheaper to marry him than pay him back. Huckert proved to be obnoxious when drinking, but he managed to control himself enough so that she didn't need to divorce or shoot him.

It seems Alice could be a bit trigger happy. In one instance, likely a little impaired by drink herself, Alice got a little anxious at her house of ill repute. It was a bit overbooked. A number of soldiers from nearby Fort Meade were on leave and had converged on her place. Alice

Alice deals cards to her friends around the table, chomping on her trademark cigar. PHOTOGRAPH COURTESY OF THE SOUTH DAKOTA HISTORICAL SOCIETY, 2008-07-07-035.

locked the doors until things settled down. The men outside weren't happy about this and started raising a ruckus. It's likely they'd had more than a few drinks under their belts. Before long, the situation escalated, and they cut the phone and electric wires. To make matters worse, the soldiers started throwing rocks through the windows. Alice wasn't one to take matters lying down. The feisty madam fired a few warning rounds through the window. As bad luck would have it (strange for Alice), she hit two of the men from the South Dakota National Guard. One man reportedly died in the hospital, while the other recovered from his wounds.

The police were at Alice's place before long and took her and her soiled doves to jail. She was charged with murder. Apparently, the judge was one of Alice's clients, and he looked upon her with some favor. At any rate, Alice dodged the shooting charges since she wasn't firing at anyone in particular and the soldiers' riotous behavior buttressed her claim of self-defense. Her girls were charged with prostitution, and Alice was charged with running a disorderly house. She paid the fines and was back in business.

At this point, Alice was a long way from being a spring chicken. She had put on a fair amount of weight, and excessive drinking and cigar smoking had taken their toll. She'd long ceased worrying about how she looked. For years, she'd taken to wearing a beat-up old hat and a men's large khaki skirt (she washed it every now and then). It had been a long time since she'd worried about her wardrobe. Her business wasn't as lively as it used to be, but she was still getting by. Prohibition added some much-needed new life to her ventures, and so did the soldiers from Fort Meade who, despite the shooting incident, still slipped over to her place to get a drink, visit a working girl, and maybe play a few games of poker. She was busted several times for bootlegging and had quite a record; however, in 1928, when she was old and in failing health, the governor of South Dakota pardoned Poker Alice on the charge of bootlegging. Governor William J. Bulow said he didn't want to send a white-haired lady to prison.

At age seventy-seven, Poker Alice Ivers underwent gallbladder surgery from which she never recovered. She was buried in Sturgis in St. Aloysius Cemetery. Her house, which was moved to Junction Avenue in Sturgis, operates as a bed-and-breakfast and is open for tours from Memorial Day to Labor Day. ൟ

6

Ella Wellington

Pining for Her Ex, She Puts a Pistol to Her Head

"I'm so happy. Oh so happy. I'll just blow my goddamn brains out!"

Having many of the luxuries the world could offer wasn't enough. The beautiful Ella put a .32-caliber handgun behind her right ear, cocked the hammer, and pulled the trigger. Gore and brains ruined the expensive bedspread and soiled some of the fancy pillows. It also ruined the political career of William R. Prynne, the Arapahoe County clerk, who was a married man.

When the story hit the newspapers, the city of Denver was in a state of shock. In her early thirties, Madam Ella Wellington was popular, beautiful, mannered, polite, and wealthy. Dressed in tasteful, expensive gowns and jewels, she was friendly and liked by those in and out of the trade. The women of the evening were especially dumbfounded. In her profession, survival was often a day-to-day struggle—emotionally, physically, and legally. A profession in this shadowy world not only meant social disenfranchisement, it also often meant that you were one trick away from being hungry, suffering in the cold, or having the hell beat out of you.

Ella was supposed to be different. She had made it, but she also had secrets.

People said Ella Wellington had ice flowing through her veins. True or not, the accusation sold her short. Ella was a perplexing woman with a complex emotional landscape. She was a business prodigy who ran one of the most successful parlor houses in the world. She appeared to have a life-work balance unusual for her profession. Maybe a handful of close friends knew about her private, personal demons. Her mantra was don't let anyone see who you truly are—and never let them see your pain. Weakness, she believed, was a chink in your fashionable armor that would inevitably be exploited. At some atavistic core, Ella was driven by a primordial desire to survive, to win, as that was all that mattered at the end of the day. The best you could expect was a return on your investment. She did, however, question what winning meant.

It's tempting to borrow a few lines from a contemporary poet of her day, Edward Arlington Robinson. His lyric poem "Richard Cory" seems apropos. While Robinson and Wellington never met (Robinson was an Easterner while Ella was from the Midwest), the two shared pessimistic and depressive natures. Each was privately disillusioned by the American dream; they both had been publicly rejected by someone they deeply loved, and neither got over the emotional scars. In some ways, Ella was a female variant of Robinson's Richard Cory. If we took Cory out and inserted Ella instead, the poem would read:

> *And [she] was rich—yes, richer than a [queen]—*
> *To make us wish that we were in [her] place*
> *So on we worked, and waited for the light,*
> *And we went without the meat, and cursed the bread.*
> *[Ella] went home and put a bullet through [her] head.*

Madam Wellington had the finest physical comforts that her profession or any profession could provide. She lived like a duchess in the lavish House of Mirrors. Unlike Richard Cory, who was a "banker's only child," Ella was a middle-class girl who acquired her fortune through her own industry. She understood how business worked but never lost "the common touch." She bought the mansion from Jennie Rogers in 1891 and grew the business.

Still, she couldn't escape brooding about her life. Publicly indifferent to the vicissitudes and ironies of her profession, Ella secretly waded through dark moods. Most women in her profession drank or used opiates to corral the gloom of their work or their lives. Ella channeled her energy into working harder and kept her despair private, focusing on business. As far as we know, she didn't drown her sorrows in alcohol, drugs, or gambling. Rather, she dove into the details of her business like an accountant. She kept her feelings bottled up tight, but she was ready to explode. Expatriated by society, she was an early (if not honorary) member of the Lost Generation.

Only to several of her closest friends—other madams—did she confide her darkest feelings and anxieties. Her rants might have been something like, "Ella Bouse, what have you done?" She used her married name; she'd run away from her old life but never forgotten her family. She realized intellectually that you can never go home again—especially in a Victorian culture that cast women statically as either good or bad. Women were pasted as asexual like the Virgin Mary or evil like Eve, the temptress who sold her birthright for a "mess of pottage" and triggered the Fall. Emotionally, Ella thought she could live with how she had spun her life, but she realized that she might have miscalculated. The primordial need to survive by growing her bank account to achieve worldly success had not made her happy. A few years after her death, Freud might have called her disease manic-depression; today, we might call her bipolar.

Whatever her condition, Ella learned that what other people thought of her wasn't as important as what she thought of herself. Her success as a brilliant entrepreneur in a difficult business milieu was hollow. Learning how to make money and how to be happy are not the same thing.

We are forced to fast-forward through her life since all we have are highlights and hints here and there. It would've been fascinating if she'd left a personal journal. We do have newspaper clippings and observations from several of her friends and business associates, but so much is laced with speculation. Ella was a private woman. In introspective moments, she thought she had failed as a wife, mother, and human being.

We know from newspaper accounts that her marriage ended badly. Before venturing into prostitution, she'd fallen madly in love. She adored the man she married, as well as his children. She felt she had a rare chance to be happy; it haunted her until she pulled the trigger. Had she traded happiness for another roll of the dice, another life, wealth, or lust? Or had an emotional trauma, something she didn't understand, leave her disconnected?

Depression and mental illness in the nineteenth century were no respecters of class or situation; even those with a wonderful family were at risk. Ella didn't wear her darkest moods on her sleeve. Like venereal disease, mental illness was not something you talked about openly. You only dealt with when it became a crisis, when it was too late. Mental illness was her private tragedy, an illness that neither she nor society understood—or knew how to deal with. She likely had no way to explain it or even voice her moods. She let it get the better of her, and it beat her up. She came from a pull-yourselves-up-by-your-bootstraps culture. In the West, a work ethic was valued. No one kept a list of handy statistics for us to quote, but in the West suicide rates were higher than we might think—mental illness was mostly self-medicated: excessive amounts of coffee (for the caffeine boost), alcohol, opiates (which were legal, cheaper than alcohol, and accessible), or death.

A newspaper reporter wrote, "Fred Bouse drove his wife from his home in Omaha because of her sins; Ella went to Salt Lake with her paramour, Samuel Cross." This might be taken at face value, but there is surely more to the story. Considering that this was written in her obituary, the assumption was that *she* had fallen into sin, which might have been the case. The article is a tidy checkbox for cause and effect, but there could be other factors to consider. It was a man's world in a day of double standards. Yes, Ella ran off with Samuel Cross. In Salt Lake City, she and Cross split up. She took the name of Wellington. In 1889, she moved to Denver and became a successful madam. But was her infidelity a weak moment? Was it a reckless manic episode? Was it in response to her husband's infidelity? Was it her way of dealing with depression? Was the marriage unhappy or abusive? Did Samuel manufacture a story to get rid of her? Or was it old-fashioned wanderlust?

WEL DENVER DIRECTORY. WEL 1039

Wellington Ella Miss, r 1942 Market.
Wellington F T Mrs, r 1619 Champa.
Wellington Herbert D, r 2215 Stout.
Wellington Herbert D Jr, clk, r 2215 Stout.
Wellman Fred E. clk Mather Brokerage & Com Co. r Berkeley.
☞See also Welles.
Wells Albert, asst engineer Steam Engine Co No 8, r 19 24th av.
Wells Alexander S, R R contractor, r 148 6th, Highlands.
Wells Alice E Mrs, hair dresser, r 720 13th.
Wells Allan T, genl frt agt D & R G R R, 311 Equitable Bldg, r 1330 S 14th.
Wells Andrew, stone mason, r rear 1644 Pennsylvania av.
Wells Benjamin F, dairyman, r 4609 Mouat av, Elyria.
Wells Benjamin T, 327 16th, r 1567 Emerson av.
Wells Charles B, clk Tramway Co, r 1335 Downing av.
Wells Charles E, butcher, r 1221 California.
Wells Charles H (C H Wells & Co), r 1333 Evans.
Wells Charles H, photographer, 1126 15th.
Wells Charles N, driver Denver Cons Laundry Co. r 460 Santa Fe av.
Wells Clayton B Rev, pastor Pilgrim Congregational Church, r 4643 Josephine, Elyria.
Wells Charles W Rev, pastor First United Brethren Church, r 103 26th av.
Wells C E, conductor City Cable Ry.
Wells C H & Co (C H Wells and G M Eastman), pianos and organs, 327 16th.
Wells Earl C, plumber, r 1747 Champa.
Wells Ebenezer T (Wells, Taylor & Taylor), r Hotel L'Imperiale.
Wells Edward C, clk National Pump & Machinery Co, r 825 Arlington.
Wells Edward D, conductor Tramway Co, r 32, 334 Gallup av.
Wells Edward P Rev, sec Westminister University, r 424 Garnet, Highlands.
Wells Eli, lab Metropole Stables, r 18, 2033 Curtis.
Wells Emma Mrs, r 46 W Maple.
Wells Eunice Miss, teacher, r 4609 Mouat av, Elyria.
WELLS, FARGO & CO'S EXPRESS, J T M Connor genl agt, J L Stubbs supt, 1637 Lawrence.
Wells Frank W (Wells & Fisher), r 1536 Glenarm.
Wells George S, machinist, r 571 S Water.
Wells Graham C, bkkpr, r 424 Garnet, Highlands.
Wells Harvey J, steamfitter, r 434 13th.
Wells H G Mrs, r 1864 Pennsylvania av.
Wells James A, lab, r 3925 Blake.
Wells Jason E, teamster, r 840 S Venice.
Wells John, hackman, r 1948 Broadway.
Wells Joseph, expressman, r 935 S 8th.
Wells J H Mrs, midwife, r 460 Santa Fe av.
Wells Laura A Miss, bkkpr E W Bowen, r 571 S Water.
Wells Laura D Mrs, r 571 S Water.
Wells Leonard W, County Comr, r es 16th bet Pearl and Agate av, Highlands.
Wells Mabel E Miss, r 1733 High.
Wells Marcus E, clk County Treas, r es 16th bet Pearl and Agate av, Highlands.
Wells Marilla E Miss, stenographer, r 840 S Emerson.
Wells Mary H Mrs, dressmkr, r 2439 Grant av.
Wells Mason, civil engineer, r 424 Garnet, Highlands.
Wells Matt, r 1438 Curtis.
Wells Nellie Miss, r 434 13th.
Wells Olie Mrs, r 12, 326 15th.
Wells Samuel T, real estate, r 825 Arlington.
WELLS, TAYLOR & TAYLOR (E T Wells, M F and J G Taylor), lawyers, 27 to 39 Tabor Blk, 16th cor Larimer.
Wells Theron B, r 1114 34th.
Wells Waldo E, conductor City Cable Co, r ws 3d bet Greeley and Beecher avs.
Wells Walter, plumber, r 2439 Grant av.
Wells William, carp, r 2439 Grant av.

The left column's top entry on Page 1041 of Corbett and Ballenger's 22nd Annual Denver City Directory *for 1894 lists a Miss Ella Wellington residing at 1942 Market Street, which was Jennie Rogers' famed House of Mirrors.* IMAGE COURTESY OF DENVER PUBLIC LIBRARY WESTERN HISTORY COLLECTION.

Ella quickly broke into the inner circle of Denver's brothels and became friends with the proprietors, which was quite rare. It was a thick glass ceiling because prostitution was a cutthroat business, and it paid to be suspicious. Her ability to function speaks highly of her people skills, management skills, and business acumen. She was a rare individual with talent who could make command decisions and be upwardly mobile without alienating or threatening her colleagues, competitors, clients, or employees. She understood the working aspects of the business, but she also understood the accounts and bookkeeping aspects that helped keep it profitable. She was an effective negotiator who grasped the importance of branding and advertising and was able to prosper.

The economy in the region faced a major setback when the Sherman Silver Purchase Act was repealed in 1893 and the government stopped buying silver. Almost overnight, the silver industry busted and the economy sputtered. Wealthy businessmen and miners were instantly insolvent, including the flamboyant millionaire and one-time U.S. senator Horace A. Tabor, aka the Bonanza King of Leadville. (Tabor died of appendicitis six years after the silver crash, and his second wife, Elizbeth "Baby Doe" McCourt ended up living as a pauper in a tool shed at the Matchless mining claim for thirty years.)

Ella thought of killing herself many times. In fact, she tried to take her life more than once. We don't know the details, but it was common knowledge among her close circle of friends. She was more fragile and on the edge than she or her close friends realized. One casual comment could cause an emotional avalanche. No one, including Ella, realized how fast she had hit the cumulative effect of no exit. She decided "not to be" because she couldn't take the slings and arrows her mind was shooting at her. As we look at the last two days of her life, we see the stage she was playing on. Let us try to re-create her final evening on earth.

As was customary, elite madams like Ella threw exclusive parties for top clients and high rollers. On July 26, 1894, she was hosting a lavish dinner party with haute cuisine, fine wine, dancing, and music. Madams in high-end brothels did this to advertise their house and its "assets" and to host their finest customers. Establishments like hers were not only brothels; they were elite social clubs, where men gathered to drink, smoke, shoot billiards, and conduct business. Ella was elegantly attired as the belle of her own ball. She wore a $2,000 diamond necklace, ruby rings, and an expensively tailored silk dress that was tightly fitted and decked with pointed lace.

Throughout the evening, there was drinking and merrymaking as guests dropped in and out. If you were wealthy, you were welcome. After midnight, a group of successful businessmen from Omaha arrived. To Ella's surprise, one of the men was an "old friend." More specifically, he was a close friend of both Ella and her ex-husband when they had been a couple. He seemed aware of their marital problems, and the assumption was they had other mutual friends, too. After the initial "fancy meeting you here" small talk, they caught up on what had happened over the past few years, chatting like alums at a reunion.

At some point in the later hours of the night, as the party got smaller, they talked about her former husband and how her two stepchildren were doing. Her old friend, probably a bit impaired by drink and missing some of his usual social filters, said too much. He talked in detail about her former husband and how he was doing well financially. He told Ella that her ex-husband had met a wonderful new woman who was the love of his life and they had married—a match made in heaven. Then Ella asked about the children. Her friend explained how they loved their new mother—they were well adjusted, now that they were in a stable environment.

Ella appeared to have been in perfect emotional control the entire evening. But this was the wave that took her by surprise. Her ex-husband doing well was one thing, but she had surely hoped the children still missed and loved her. She didn't want to be replaced so easily. Ella uncharacteristically dropped her wine glass. She said something about how happy she was for them. Observers in the room said they felt a chill. At this point, the party was over.

Wearing diamonds and an expensive dress meant nothing. Ella felt how useless and shallow her life had been. She'd reached a pinnacle of financial success, but she missed her children more than ever. Her past was her past, a guarded secret. She was all about control, but some things you cannot control. As she walked up the stairs to her room, she reportedly turned on the steps and said, perhaps to the exiting guests, "I'm so happy. Oh so happy. I'll just blow my goddamn brains out!"

Supposedly she said, "Oh so happy" several times as she walked up the stairs. There was a drunken man asleep in her bed—William R. Prynne, the Arapahoe County clerk. He was an on-off lover who wouldn't leave his family for Ella. Presumably, he awoke at the sound of Ella's gun going off. Which is about all that he could later tell the coroner and, presumably, his wife.

Ella's funeral was elaborate and expensive, but the story isn't quite over. Apparently her death was too much for an admirer named Fredrick N. Sturges. To demonstrate his love, it's said that he slept on top of her grave for several nights and couldn't be consoled. He then bought the plot next to hers. Within weeks, he was dead from an overdose of opiates. He left instructions to be buried next to the woman he loved. ൴

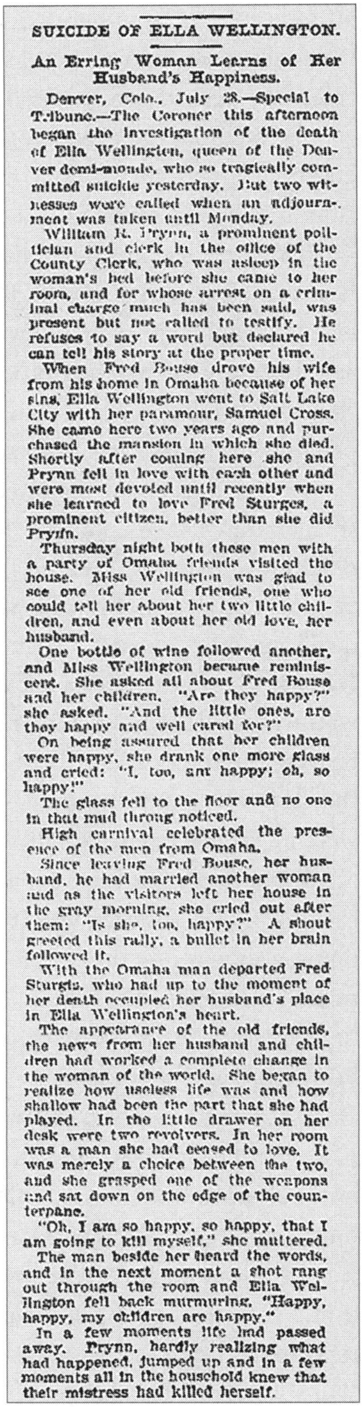

SUICIDE OF ELLA WELLINGTON.

An Erring Woman Learns of Her Husband's Happiness.

Denver, Colo., July 28.—Special to Tribune.—The Coroner this afternoon began the investigation of the death of Ella Wellington, queen of the Denver demi-monde, who so tragically committed suicide yesterday. But two witnesses were called when an adjournment was taken until Monday.

William R. Prynn, a prominent politician and clerk in the office of the County Clerk, who was asleep in the woman's bed before she came to her room, and for whose arrest on a criminal charge much has been said, was present but not called to testify. He refuses to say a word but declared he can tell his story at the proper time.

When Fred Bouse drove his wife from his home in Omaha because of her sins, Ella Wellington went to Salt Lake City with her paramour, Samuel Cross. She came here two years ago and purchased the mansion in which she died. Shortly after coming here she and Prynn fell in love with each other and were most devoted until recently when she learned to love Fred Sturges, a prominent citizen, better than she did Prynn.

Thursday night both these men with a party of Omaha friends visited the house. Miss Wellington was glad to see one of her old friends, one who could tell her about her two little children, and even about her old love, her husband.

One bottle of wine followed another, and Miss Wellington became reminiscent. She asked all about Fred Bouse and her children. "Are they happy?" she asked. "And the little ones, are they happy and well cared for?"

On being assured that her children were happy, she drank one more glass and cried: "I, too, am happy; oh, so happy!"

The glass fell to the floor and no one in that mad throng noticed.

High carnival celebrated the presence of the men from Omaha.

Since leaving Fred Bouse, her husband, he had married another woman and as the visitors left her house in the gray morning, she cried out after them: "Is she, too, happy?" A shout greeted this rally, a bullet in her brain followed it.

With the Omaha man departed Fred Sturgis, who had up to the moment of her death occupied her husband's place in Ella Wellington's heart.

The appearance of the old friends, the news from her husband and children had worked a complete change in the woman of the world. She began to realize how useless life was and how shallow had been the part that she had played. In the little drawer on her desk were two revolvers. In her room was a man she had ceased to love. It was merely a choice between the two, and she grasped one of the weapons and sat down on the edge of the counterpane.

"Oh, I am so happy, so happy, that I am going to kill myself," she muttered.

The man beside her heard the words, and in the next moment a shot rang out through the room and Ella Wellington fell back murmuring, "Happy, happy, my children are happy."

In a few moments life had passed away. Prynn, hardly realizing what had happened, jumped up and in a few moments all in the household knew that their mistress had killed herself.

A July 29, 1894, Salt Lake Tribune *column summed up Ella's final act with the headline: "Suicide of Ella Wellington, An Erring Woman Learns of Her Husband's Happiness."* IMAGE COURTESY OF THE LIBRARY OF CONGRESS.

MOLLIE PRICE

The Metal in the Madam's Corset Turned a Bullet . . . Part of Her Ear Was Bitten Off in a Fight

Mollie Price (sometimes Molly May) was a bawdy veteran of the Dakotas, Wyoming, and Pueblo, Colorado, before settling in Leadville. She grew up in a tough world and understood the laws of the jungle. Anecdotal history has it that she lost part of her ear in a rough-and-tumble fight with another woman over a man named Jim. Her adversary bit it off. In another instance, two men fighting for Mollie's affections got into a bit of gunplay, with Mollie a not-so-innocent bystander. A stray bullet hit her, but a metal rib in her corset deflected the lead, saving her life.

Scandal, disturbing the peace, and owning the most lavish house in town all served as good advertising for Mollie. She was a savvy businesswoman who could turn a profit in a brothel. She was not afraid to exchange shots with a rival madam or have one of the silver barons, perhaps the wealthy Horace Tabor, as a silent partner in a lavish brothel venture.

Mollie was the reigning madam in wicked Leadville. After fifteen hard years on the line, she died suddenly in 1887. Her funeral—held, naturally, in her brothel—was ostentatious. Her estate was worth more than $35,000, a tidy sum (nearly $1 million in today's dollars). Mollie's obituary read: "She was a woman who with all her bad qualities, was much given to charity and was always willing to help the poor and unfortunate."

7

Laura Bell McDaniel

The Colorful Courtesan of Colorado City and Her Tragic Death

Laura Bell knew Billy the Kid in New Mexico before Pat Garrett shot him. Billy's cousin Rhody "Dusty" McCarty would become a close friend. Vagabond author John "Prairie Dog" O'Byrne—who wrote Pikes Peak or Bust and Historical Sketches of the Wild West*—would be a lifelong friend, soulmate, and lover.*

Laura Bell worked the madam trade for thirty years in some of the wildest towns in Colorado's gold country: Salida, Cripple Creek, and Colorado City. She hired Bob Ford, the man who shot Jesse James, as a faro dealer at the Nickel Plate Saloon.

Laura Bell had millionaire clients, was married three times, and—unlike most women in her trade—was close to her family. Her daughter, sisters, nieces, nephews, mother, and husbands all lived close by. She spent most of her life in a world that ran on horses but then died in an automobile accident.

Many unanswered questions remain about her life: did Laura Bell conspire to burn down her house for the insurance settlement before she and Tom McDaniel married? Answer: probably, but we're not sure. Was Laura Bell complicit in a scheme with her new husband to set up Morgan Dunn to take the blame for arson? Answer: a lukewarm maybe-sort-of.

Did Laura Bell conspire with Tom to murder Morgan Dunn, or was it Tom's idea? Was it a crime of momentary passion, calculation, or self-defense? The shooting took place in the couple's living room, while Laura and her mother watched. Tom put five slugs in Dunn's chest. We're curious if Dunn really did make improper advances toward Laura Bell, as was claimed. Newspaper accounts were inconsistent, but then, so were Laura's and Tom's testimonies.

Laura Bell was a single mother who provided not only for her daughter, Pearl, but also for her extended family. Like her mother, Anna (her role model), Laura Bell kept her family close and cared for. They stuck together. This warm familial association sets Laura Bell apart from every other working bawdy woman in this book. Her family knew what she did for a living and accepted it. No verified pictures of Laura Bell exist, but she might have had dark, wavy hair and naturally ruddy cheeks. She was reportedly pretty, liked colorful clothes, and—as we'll see—had an adventurous spirit. Because she was in the public eye during her professional career, we have firsthand recollections, legal documents, newspaper accounts, and folklore to draw from. Details and accounts about her life naturally vary, especially regarding some of her more public adventures. This just makes her story all the more interesting.

When Robert Newton "Bob" Ford showed up in Colorado looking for work, Laura Bell hired him to deal faro at the Nickel Plate Saloon. Ford had been eking out a living selling photographs like this one as "the man who killed Jesse James." He later opened his own saloon in Creede, where he was gunned down at the age of thirty. PHOTOGRAPH COURTESY OF WIKIMEDIA.

After her family moved from Kentucky, she was born Laura Bell Horton in Buffalo Lick, Missouri, on November 27, 1861, to James and Anna Eliza Horton. The land was good and they worked hard, but the Civil War made life difficult. Her father was not listed on the 1870 census, so presumably he had died by then, perhaps killed in the war. Anna did her best to keep the farm going and remarried, so Laura Bell had half-sisters. The young lady was confident, friendly, and outgoing. She was also able to read and write.

At nineteen, a local boy named Samuel Dale caught her eye. The young couple moved West but didn't live happily ever after. There's not much known about their relationship other than that they lived in the Southwest. Ostensibly, there were times when Samuel was gone, perhaps on business, and the young wife was left by herself. Laura Bell talked about her friendship with Dusty McCarty in New Mexico and his cousin Henry McCarty, the man we know as Billy the Kid. She met Billy shortly before he was killed by Sheriff Pat Garrett in the summer of 1881. It'd be interesting to have some insight into her views on the young outlaw. Billy was no plaster saint, but he chose the wrong side in the Lincoln County War and was victimized by the press—something Laura Bell would understand in a few years.

By 1882, she was going by the name Bell Dale and resided in Salida, a thriving new rail town. Her daughter, Eva Pearl, was born in 1884, but troubles were brewing. Perhaps Samuel had a hard time being a husband or, more to the point, being Laura's husband. He had faded out of her life by the 1885 census. Laura Bell owned a small house in the respectable part of town and worked as a clerk. She invited her mother and stepsisters to join her. Her mother, now a widow, ran a boardinghouse and helped look after Pearl. Laura Bell continued this pattern for the rest of her life. She liked having her family nearby. When she took up the mantle of madamhood, they all stayed together, as unorthodox as it seemed. There must have been some interesting dinner discussions. With the exception of a niece named Little Laura, none of the family followed Laura Bell into the trade.

While clerking, Laura Bell noticed John Thomas "Tom" McDaniel, a debonair frontier dandy. He was dashing—a bit of a naughty boy—and far more exciting than her former husband. Tom was a smooth talker and likely started her thinking about fast money and "the good life." He was aware that she had a fire insurance policy. Working as a clerk was quite respectable, but it earned survival wages at best. Laura Bell may have felt financial pressure now that her mother and stepsisters were with her. She would learn that Tom was slippery, but the romance blossomed. They schemed and talked of marriage, clothes, and living in style. We don't know the details of Laura's disposition, but to a struggling single mom, a better life was no doubt alluring.

Glib Tom made the scheme sound easy, even foolproof. Anna would take Pearl, and Tom and Laura Bell would go on a vacation to Leadville. They'd be above reproach, and he'd take care of the details. After the settlement, they'd marry in style. So it went: the couple traveled to Leadville, her house burned to the ground, and Laura filed an insurance claim. They waited for the settlement. They received a check and married on April 7, 1887, after the check cleared. As her husband, Tom was now legally entitled to his share, in case Laura Bell had a change of heart.

To the surprise of those around her, Laura Bell relocated to the bad part of town. It was a puzzling move for a decent woman. Respectable eyebrows were raised; after all, she had a job, daughter, and mother nearby. Folks expected her to clear the charred ruins and rebuild. We know this move was a conscious decision on Laura Bell's part, but in a frontier town it probably looked like an act of desperation. Likely, the good residents assumed it was the corrupting influence of the shifty Tom McDaniel, whom she should never have gotten involved with in the first place. Indeed, Tom probably suggested investing in a brothel. We don't think Laura Bell was in the sporting trade yet, but the move was something she must have been considering.

In the lore surrounding this incident, Morgan Dunn has been colored as a disagreeable bully, a barroom brawler, and a womanizer; after he was shot, it came out that he had a wife back East. What we do know is that he boldly took center stage on one fateful evening. Morgan had rented a room at Laura's mother's—Anna's—boardinghouse. The couple visited Anna often, so they would've known Morgan.

With the insurance money in hand, the newlyweds planned a short vacation to Red Rocks—a honeymoon getaway southwest of

Denver. But then Laura casually mentioned to Tom that Morgan had tried to kiss her. Tom became furious, saying, "You should have killed the son of a bitch." This understandably dampened the mood between them. Distraught, they went to her mother's boardinghouse for dinner. When the couple arrived, they ran into the amorous, unrepentant, obnoxious Morgan Dunn, who was eating. This could hardly have been a surprise, since Dunn boarded there. The impertinent Dunn, without apparent provocation, became abusive, mouthy, and vulgar, threatening to kill Tom. Morgan was known as a tough man, so Tom was reluctant to engage in fisticuffs. Also, it seems Tom wasn't armed, or he'd have brandished his pistol to quell the explosive maniac. Just before physical violence occurred, Laura Bell valiantly stepped in, insisting that she and Tom leave. Understandably concerned for her mother's as well as her husband's safety, she asked her mother to come with them. The shaken trio walked back to the McDaniels' home.

After they settled down, someone discovered they'd run out of candles. Tom stepped out to buy some. The two women were talking when there was a loud, obnoxious knock on the front door. (This is starting to sound like a summer-stock melodrama, from our perspective.) The bully Dunn pushed his way in. After all that had transpired, the two women wouldn't willingly have let this lunatic into the house. Dunn escalated from obnoxious to threatening. As he was about to hit or ravish Laura Bell, Tom returned with candles. His castle was being threatened, and he had to defend it. Angry, fearful—and righteously indignant—he stepped forward.

Dunn immediately called him out—"We might as well settle it now"—and reached for his hip as if he were going for a gun. Tom pulled his pistol and fired five slugs. Dunn dropped, absorbing nearly one thousand grains of lead. If the dying man had time to cough involuntarily before expiring, blood would've oozed from his mouth. A gunshot death is not pretty, nor does it smell good. The survivors surely didn't fully register the deafening reports or the layers of heavy smoke from black powder. Even in a lively town on a Friday night, men were knocking on the front door almost at once. Tom answered, pistol in his hand. "He had no business in my house!" he said. At the same time, Anna said over and over, "Tom, why did you do that?"

The police were summoned. Rowdy behavior was common around watering holes, but normal citizens—even in the wildest towns—almost never shot someone in their living room. Investigating officials assumed the household was in shock; nowadays, we might call it cognitive dissonance—how we shield ourselves emotionally from mental trauma. Tom was arrested, and Dunn was quickly buried. Tom's case for self-defense was plausible, especially when the two women spoke of their fear and the earlier threats were confirmed. Some parts of the story didn't fit neatly (why had Anna asked Tom his reason for shooting?), but it appeared to be self-defense. Tom was acquitted.

The case eventually dropped from the news, but Dunn's wife and other family members asked questions. The case was retried in the press. Some thought there were possible connections between Dunn and the fire that had destroyed Laura Bell's old building, but there was never enough proof for further legal action. Articles circulated that Dunn was unarmed and had a broken collarbone. Other suppositions came out, suggesting varying levels of Dunn's involvement in the arson plot. The *Salida Semi-Weekly Mail* was critical.

It was foolish, but to try and clear their names, the couple agreed to an interview. On May 20, 1887, the *Salida Semi-Weekly Mail* crucified them in print. The paper implied that the shooting wasn't an act of self-defense but rather an execution. Fissures in the couple's story were opening. Laura Bell and Tom insisted that Dunn had taken his coat off, that she had put it on her bed. But wait, if his coat was off, wouldn't they have seen that he wasn't wearing a gun on his hip? And why would the lady of the house have politely offered to take a man's coat after he forced his way in? Readers inferred motives. The couple insisted that Anna got her story wrong. Also, it looked like there was previous collusion and reasonable evidence that pointed to Dunn as the alleged arsonist. The *Salida Semi-Weekly Mail* sold a lot of papers.

There was no strongly incriminating evidence, so opinions roughly split into three camps. The first concluded that Dunn was unstable and had inappropriately stalked and tried to steal a kiss from a decent woman. At his boardinghouse—a public place and in front of witnesses—he'd been disorderly, abusive, and threatening. If Laura

Bell hadn't stepped in at her mother's place, who knows what could've happened. Not wanting to push the unstable man, the reasonable and prudent family had left the boardinghouse to defuse the situation. Later that evening, Dunn had burst into their home with malicious intent. There was probable cause for using deadly force. The second perspective was that Dunn had been set up. He was a volatile man who had played into a clever calculation. He'd been involved with the conniving couple in a conspiracy to commit arson and had then been marginalized by them. He'd been skillfully baited, his predictable buttons pushed. He'd been killed to shut him up, or so Tom could keep Dunn's share of the insurance money. The third set of opinions saw no one as being that clever; they were likely all guilty—a bunch of opportunistic criminals. This had been a crime of passion and Dunn a last-minute patsy.

This event appears to have been the beginning of the end of the relationship between Laura Bell and Tom. Maybe Laura Bell saw sides of him that she wasn't prepared to accept, or she was unhappy with herself for being part of a roughly drafted script whose ending she hadn't foreseen. Laura Bell distanced herself from Tom. In the future, she would have serious lovers and one more husband, but Laura Bell never let anyone have this kind of control over her again. Tom left and didn't come back.

Laura Bell used her money to go into the madam business in the bad part of town. Then in 1888, she relocated to Colorado City, a wild town that embraced the seven deadly sins. Laura Bell was a long way from Eden, but her family was with her, making her a professional exception. Bold and flamboyant, she spent nearly thirty years as the "Courtesan of Colorado City."

The cavalier stories of Laura Bell and John "Prairie Dog" O'Byrne are among the most celebrated in Western mythology. Their antics punctuated their way of life. They would live to see the frontier slip away, like pure Rocky Mountain spring water. Even though they cupped their hands as tightly as they could, it leaked through. Unconventional and unrestrained, both Laura Bell and John were social outcasts who fought against domesticating boundaries and the decaying tenants of Victorianism. They were fated to usher in the age of jazz, speakeasies, and modernism, but they remained outcasts because their contemplations were neither fashionable nor existential. Rather, their introspections were too rooted in wilderness and frontier hedonism. Their adventures seem almost carefree, perhaps dreamlike, when juxtaposed with the coming decades of world wars, mustard gas, influenza, genocide, and nuclear bombs.

While the tales of the Courtesan of Colorado and Prairie Dog are joyously stretched, mixed, and matched, the relationship was in fact real. John O'Byrne was her client, her soulmate, her lover—and a dear friend. He was the "Peter Pan of the Prairie," although everyone called him Prairie Dog. It may be true that he never quite grew up, whatever growing up means, but it's hard to blame him for making the West his Neverland. He earned his nickname honestly, because he kept prairie dogs for pets. He generally had one of his "dawgs" in his wagon to show clients. He had an infectious fascination with flora and fauna. He was a lousy poet, but it would be unfair to label John O'Byrne's written work as unsophisticated or sophomoric. Naturally curious, he never lost his childlike sense of wonder, which was something Laura Bell loved about him. He stopped and smelled the sagebrush. His enthusiasm made his book *Pikes Peak or Bust and Historical Sketches of the Wild West*—self-published in 1922—delightful. Structurally, it's a mess; he's no Mark Twain or William Dean Howells. However, if you look at his book as a collection of rambling, disorganized, and episodic sketches that are both laments and celebrations, it's a wonderful slice of life, an unpretentious snapshot. (In my lectures, I refer to his essays as "Prairie Dog Logic.") This happy-go-lucky, folksy fellow talked about the West that was vanishing in front of him.

John was born in 1862 in the Midwest and grew up in Kansas. In his wanderings, he saw Indians, buffalo, gunfights, hangings, and goldfields. He drove stage and worked for the railroad. He talked about honky-tonks, whorehouses, and gambling. As a cowboy philosopher, he paid special tribute to his friendship with Laura Bell. He fell in love with the Rocky Mountains and never got over it. Ever a storyteller and teacher, John made his living driving a wagon, shuttling gold-seekers, miners, and tourists. He loved nothing more than showing off Colorado, driving visitors to various places of interest and providing commentary as they rolled along. Once, he took a stagecoach full of passengers to the summit of Pikes Peak, waxing eloquent from top to bottom. He also ran a thriving business taking men from "dry" Colorado Springs to the vices, bars, and fleshpots of Colorado City. Prairie Dog liked to drink, gamble, and visit the ladies with ticking meters. He was better at drinking and entertaining women than gambling; he was fond of "bucking the tiger" and playing faro, but then scrambled to pay off his debts.

In 1888, John trained two elk, Thunder and Buttons, to pull his wagon. It was quite a novelty. Laura Bell and Prairie Dog would go for long drives together, sitting side by side and snuggling as they flew over the dirt road. They enjoyed seeing how fast they could get to Colorado Springs, three miles away. Occasionally, they'd draw curses when they didn't slow down within city limits. The curiosity of two harnessed elk going too fast caused horses and drivers of fancy carriages to bolt or jolt—upsetting well-heeled ladies and gentlemen. Prairie Dog wrote, "I took many pains to spend all my cash, and / I drove through the street with Laura Bell by my side— / A span of elk, how fine we did ride." Apparently, John would now and then get the modern equivalent of a drunk- or reckless-driving ticket. He occasionally spent the night in jail for his robust driving habits.

John O'Byrne, left, holds the reins on Thunder and Buttons, the elk he trained to pull a wagon or buggy. PHOTOGRAPH COURTESY OF WIKITREE.

When they met, Laura Bell and John were in their late twenties. They went on real dates—not some pretended assignations in a whorehouse, clouded by perfume, gaudy-prettiness, makeup, and coquettish flirtations for dollars. They enjoyed each other immensely and understood and appreciated each other's vulnerabilities without many demands. Both in their own ways were social oddities, perhaps hiding from their lives for a few moments, like Dimmesdale and Hester in *The Scarlet Letter* when they meet in the forest. For Laura Bell, it was a pleasant change to make real small talk with a friend; she wasn't on a shelf like a piece of fruit in a market. When Laura Bell's mother died, Prairie Dog likely consoled her. They enjoyed their elk-drawn drives until John was forced by circumstances (probably gambling debts) to take a higher-paying job. He moved away but came back to visit.

The drama of being a madam never ceased. Laura Bell's employees needed constant attention and were often emotionally unstable, suicidal, or addicted to a substance—not to mention the never-ending fears of pregnancy and disease. She was successfully located in Colorado City, with occasional ventures to Cripple Creek. She moved often, opening and closing venues at different locations, rebuilding or running different houses concurrently. Some of her Colorado City locations included 611 Washington Avenue, 615 South Sixth Street, 609 Washington Avenue, 410 Grand Avenue, and 421 Grand Avenue. Her business model was typical. There was a lot of turnover and no end to the need for managerial decisions, such as scaling houses up or down (to facilitate the number of employees), remodeling, and upgrades. Equally important were rezoning, fines, and license structures, which were always in flux. A moving target was harder to pin down. Bribing police and local government officials was also a constant expenditure. Several times, Laura Bell moved to Cripple Creek to escape political pressure, or she ran a house in each town.

By 1909, it was no longer business as usual. *The Colorado City Iris* said, "She was the most influential sinner of them all." Pearl moved to Denver, perhaps at her mother's insistence, to insulate her from the coming storm. We know that Pearl (who lived into the 1960s) had frequent visits from Laura Bell in 1909. The Courtesan of Colorado City had become the focus for the township's collective sins, and this would prove to be a difficult year. Mayor Ira Foote issued an edict that all prostitutes had ten days to get the hell out of Dodge. This would also be known as the year of the Crimson Fire; a blaze that started in a low-end bawdy house burned a good section of the red-light district. Laura Bell's place, the Trilby, was consumed. Many think the blaze was started intentionally. Several vocal preachers had predicted that the wrath of God would fall upon the sinners. The fire occurred in January during freezing temperatures, so it was difficult to fight. Many residents of the red-light district suffered from the elements. Laura Bell built a new house, this time with bricks. She called it the Mansions. This brazen move upset her detractors. She refused to go. Fines increased as the sin district was put under a microscope, and she had to be careful.

Laura Bell was ready to tie the matrimonial knot again in 1911, this time with her friend Herbert N. Berg, a newspaper editor with the *Colorado Springs Gazette Telegraph*. His specialty was finance, and his advice was always good. The union of the aging madam and the aging newspaperman turned more than a few heads. It was a bold move, but that was Laura Bell. Herbert thought the fervor amusing. But this marriage gave Laura Bell an added layer of insulation in the larger political scheme, as her new husband had powerful connections. As a humorous aside, both Laura Bell and Herbert fibbed about their ages on their marriage certificate. Laura Bell was hitting the half-century mark, certainly not in her thirties as she claimed. After the nuptial, she hotly ran an ad in her husband's paper, stating that she had "furnished rooms"—a euphemism among the red-light set indicating that she was still in business.

On January 1, 1916, Colorado became the first state to embrace Prohibition, four years before the law passed nationally. This boosted Laura Bell's anxieties and decreased her sphere of influence, as did Herbert's unexpected death. With the new law, alcohol—a lucrative part of her business—became a serious issue. The noose was tightening as the Conformist Movement put additional pressure on law enforcement to shut down tenderloin districts to curb illegal drinking. At the same time, Colorado Springs annexed Colorado City. Colorado Springs had always had strict morality laws. Laura Bell became a symbol, a target. In November 1917, the police were on her doorstep with a warrant. They searched her house and quickly found bottles of expensive liquor that had been "reported as stolen." It was an obvious setup. The police knew exactly where to look. Arrested for receiving stolen goods, Laura Bell's bail was set at an outrageous $1,500. Her trial date was set for January 17, 1918. The shameless madam hired two expensive lawyers, Jake Orr and W. D. Lombard, to represent her; a positive outcome looked tenuous. The trial was a long chain of detectives testifying against her. But in the end, her old friend Dusty McCarty testified on her behalf, telling the court the liquor had been planted by some suspicious folks who had come by the house. Laura was acquitted. This was a stinging blow for the police force. They'd thought they had an open-and-shut case.

Relieved and needing a vacation, Laura Bell decided to go to Denver to visit her family. She had a 1916 Mitchell touring car that she loved. With her niece Little Laura and Dusty, who'd been blinded in a mining accident, they headed out. Dusty, of course, had saved her, and she was grateful.

Laura Bell proudly owned a Mitchell touring car like this one, but it proved to be her undoing.
PHOTOGRAPH COURTESY OF THE SEATTLE MUNICIPAL ARCHIVES.

Now, if you enjoy conspiracy theories, this might prove noteworthy. They were traveling in Colorado in the winter, and the roads could've been icy. With Little Laura driving, they hit the dizzying speed of almost forty miles per hour, skidded, lost control, and crashed. Little Laura was killed instantly. Laura Bell was critically injured and hospitalized with internal injuries before she died. Dusty was miraculously uninjured. How do we know these details? Police detectives reported the accident because they saw it occur. What were they doing on a country road? Were they following the touring car on purpose to make a point. Did they run the car off the road as an act of vengeance because of the acquittal? Did the police car pass and swerve, making Little Laura panic? Were they following her, or was it chance? Many theorized that the police were responsible for the accident.

At the age of fifty-six, Laura Bell was buried in Fairview Cemetery in Colorado Springs. Her estate went to her daughter, Pearl.

Laura Bell was buried with her niece, Laura Pearson, in Fairview Cemetery in Colorado Springs. PHOTOGRAPH COURTESY OF RON WEST.

LOU BUNCH

The Large Queen of Central City

Her name was Louisa, but everyone called her Big Lou. The portly madam weighed over 300 pounds and was certainly the shadiest lady in Central City. She's fondly remembered as the "Queen of Gunnell Hill." Madam Lou loved baseball and supported a local team. Rumor has it that Lou and the mayor were caught in a love nest. The mayor's wife, incensed by the betrayal, pushed the adulterers' brass bed out into the street—and Lou was apparently still in the bed. After a moment, the angry wife decided to push the bed, with the madam on it, to the edge of the city limits. Considering the weight of a brass bed, the mattress, and the madam, this must have been quite a feat. (Today, Central City holds bed races on Lou Bunch Day in June to honor the madam.)

But Lou wasn't all bad. During an epidemic, Madam Bunch closed her business and with her shady ladies tended to the sick miners. When Colorado enacted Prohibition in 1916, Lou closed her house in Central City and moved in with Mattie Silks (for whom she had worked in the 1880s) in Denver and cared for her until Silks died in early 1929.

8

Laura Evens

Madam of Five Decades

YES, HER CAREER SPANNED FIFTY YEARS. She knew Mattie Silks on Denver's Market Street, worked in Leadville, and opened a business in Salida. In her younger days, Laura was famous for her drunken antics. She collected rococo dolls and drank whiskey straight, although a housekeeper said she preferred champagne. She was a chain smoker who rolled her own but used a cigarette holder. She didn't want people to curse around her, but she'd swear like an angry mule skinner.

Laura managed to stay thin despite her favorite food being dollar-sized pancakes—well-cooked but not burned. She once smiled at several "social reformers" who tried to correct the error of her ways; she told the do-gooders she was already going to hell, so they needn't bother. Slipping the evangelists some bills, Laura told them to carry on their good work, because they might help some younger woman who wasn't as far gone as she was. When she died in 1953, the Denver Post *devoted half a page to her, saying she belonged to another era.*

Laura and a few friends once attended the Ringling Bros. Circus when it came to Leadville. Circuses were a big deal, so the ladies did a fair amount of drinking as they toasted the parade of exotic animals. Laura appreciated the tease, the enticement of the big ring, and the promised show, but mostly she had an incredible fascination for chariots and insisted that she get to drive one. There are a variety of accounts about what happened next in the mythology, each with its own twist.

At any rate, she got her wish. Laura bribed, borrowed, or rented one of the precarious carts and reportedly rushed about like a bellicose warrior. At breakneck speed, she charged down Harrison Avenue, zipping past the row of crib houses to the cheers of the festive men and women on the streets. Impaired by drink, she crashed the Roman two-wheeler into a pole in front of the Vendome Hotel. Laura catapulted out, dazed and confused but unhurt. She started laughing. We're told that a nearby policeman arrested her for drunk and reckless driving, or perhaps stealing a chariot or endangerment. However, before he hauled her off to jail, a good-natured "client" stepped in and spoke to the officer. Since no one was hurt, he said, he'd return the chariot and horses to the circus in time for the next show and would pay any damages.

Thanks to her longevity and notoriety, we know much more about Laura Evens than we do about many Old West madams. But one detail remains a mystery: the spelling of her last name. Many sources cite it as Evans, surely a more common spelling of this surname. When asked about this in the 1970s, her attorney, Fred M. Mazzulla, insisted that it was Evens. Presumably, her attorney would know such things, so for this account, Evens it is.

A hellraiser in her youth, the effervescent Laura was wild and daring. She loved to dance and sing. She also had a stinging sense of humor. Ever the prankster, Laura once bet $50 that she could crash a masquerade ball and not be noticed. She went as a nun. The photograph of Laura as such is worth a thousand words. She collected her bet, playing the role to perfection. The double entendre wasn't lost on her—or seemingly on her friends—since *nun* is a slang term for a whore. (In Shakespeare's *Hamlet*, the young prince tells Ophelia, "Get thee to a nunnery." Hamlet was telling her she was a whore and needed to go to a whorehouse.)

Laura made a convincing nun for a masquerade ball. PHOTOGRAPH COURTESY OF THE FRED M. MAZZULLA COLLECTION, HISTORY COLORADO.

Though known for her revelry and for embracing an epicurean lifestyle, Laura had dark shadows in her past that she almost never talked about. Perhaps the most poignant was how, as a teenaged wife and mother, she deserted her family. Laura might have been born on May 31, 1874, but that date is unconfirmed. We know she was brought up in a prosperous Southern home and was educated at a Catholic school—a young lady of privilege. Laura took voice and dance lessons like a proper, budding debutante. Later, she commented that her good voice cost her father a lot of money.

She married and assumed that she'd have a storybook life, but something went wrong when she and her young husband were living in St. Louis. In an interview after Laura's death, one of her close friends filled in a few details based on a conversation she'd had with Laura while playing pan—a card game like rummy—and drinking and talking until dawn. Laura mentioned that she'd fled her marriage because she was so unhappy, although she didn't elaborate on why. She bought a one-way ticket to Denver and got on the train with her baby, Lucille. However, taking care of her baby was more difficult than she'd expected, and it opened her eyes. Apparently, she knew nothing about child care. She was unsure of when to feed her little girl, how to change diapers, or even how to calm her when she screamed or cried. Motherhood, Laura commented, was too difficult and heightened her anxieties and frustrations. Laura said, almost as an aside, that she was certain she wasn't designed to live a domestic life. Worse, she didn't feel connected to her infant, although her daughter would later be an off-and-on part of her life and Laura would support her financially.

Laura's husband followed her to Denver, but their marital relationship wasn't salvageable. Laura disconnected and started over. In our day, some might look at her behavior through a neurological lens and use words like *self-preservation, borderline personality disorder, fight or flight, or emotional inhibition*. But in her day, sadly, there were few emotional safety nets. Not to put too fine a point on Laura Evens, but in the 1800s, a woman could be declared insane for "being too educated." While this seems far-fetched, consider an 1875 book called *Sex in Education or, a Fair Chance for Girls*. The author, a medical doctor named Edward Clarke, suggested that if young women were educated like young men, the result would likely be "hysteria," a catch-all term for any number of mental illnesses. Education, Clarke continued, could also result in a "uterine disease" and "derangements of the nervous system."

Doing the best she could, presumably, Laura self-medicated by pulling the cork out of a bottle, bingeing on strong drink, and being a good-time party girl. She worked on Denver's Market Street during the early days of her career, but a regulated brothel life like that—working for a mistress like Mattie Silks or Jennie Rogers—proved to be too stifling. After the Denver Strangler killed at least three prostitutes in the late 1890s, Market Street was referred to as "Stranglers Row." Laura desperately needed a new venue with more personal freedom. From a business perspective, she thought she could make more money on her own. Furthermore, she liked to make fun of the older Market Street parlors, saying all they offered were "old ladies." She made her way to Leadville, known as the "City in the Clouds," where she continued to earn her deserved reputation as a merry prankster. To say the least, Laura was a spirited young lady who drank too much and played hard. During these restless Leadville years, the daring Laura sowed wild oats, and her legend grew. Besides her adventure as a rash chariot driver, there are two other tales we'll look at: Laura at the Ice Palace and Laura as a union buster.

In its heyday, Leadville offered boundless opportunities for mischief and revenue for a woman of Laura's inclinations. PHOTOGRAPH BY JOHN DUER, COURTESY OF THE U.S. GEOLOGICAL SURVEY.

When the price of silver dropped in the 1890s, Colorado's economy tanked. Leadville was hit hard, losing 70 percent of its population. The town came up with a bold plan: build a giant ice palace and bring in tourist dollars. They hired a famous architect to design a frozen palace wonderland. The project called for 5,000 tons of ice, 180,000 board feet of lumber, and 250 men, who would work around the clock. The project was completed in a month. The frozen doors opened in December 1895. Not only was the place fun to visit for a working girl on holiday, it was also a great place to advertise. This icy fairyland would draw a quarter of a million visitors before the spring thaw in March 1896.

That holiday season, the smell of popcorn and the magic of Christmas filled the air. The Norman-inspired palace was the largest ice structure ever built. It had electric lights and a restaurant, skating rink, dance floor, and ballroom. There were ninety-foot towers, gambling parlors, drinking places, theaters, toboggan runs, roses, and a merry-go-round. Trout were even frozen into great blocks of ice. Admission cost fifty cents for grownups and twenty-five cents for kids. (Today, adjusting for inflation, that's about $16 per adult and $8 per kid.)

The wonder of Leadville's Ice Palace drew visitors from across Colorado. PHOTOGRAPH BY WILLIAM HENRY JACKSON, COURTESY OF THE LIBRARY OF CONGRESS, LC-USZ62-104511.

Several accounts exist of how the evening of Laura's visit unfolded. One has Laura and a few of her Leadville friends "borrowing" a Santa-style sleigh. The naughty ladies were more than halfway inebriated with spirits before they arrived. Somehow, a telephone pole *mysteriously* jumped in the way. Laura, the driver (likely seeing double), swerved, and the sleigh smashed into the palace's front wall. The jolly whores tumbled or stumbled into the palace, making a raucous entrance.

Laura's recollection of events differed. She said she and her boon companion—a fellow named Broomtail Charlie—dressed up for an evening on the town and hired a sleigh so that they could arrive at the palace in style. As they pulled up to the entrance, the horse bolted, spooked by the bright lights, loud music, glow of the ice, and crowds. Confused, the poor beast mistakenly burst into the lobby. Laura said, "He kicked the hell out of our sleigh and broke an ice shaft as he ran away." She added, "The animal ruined a pillar [and] busted up some exhibits." The couple apparently weren't worried about the horse, since they went on celebrating. Laura noted that the horse found its way home.

In another famous tale from the Leadville lineup, Laura was credited with breaking the back of a labor union. Collective bargaining and labor were touchy subjects in gold country. Everyone had a strong opinion. There were loud disputes over wages, safety conditions, and organizing labor during this era. The mining industry had shifted from individuals roaming the hillsides to large operations, but it remained a dangerous occupation. Talks between working men and management got especially heated at the Maid of Erin Mine. The labor "rabble-rousers" called for a strike, and many of the men of the Maid walked. However, enough stayed to keep the mine going. The owners didn't want a shooting war—at least not yet—but they needed to pay the workers.

Management asked the congenial Laura Evens if she could come to the rescue. Could the good madam get past the striking miners blockading the entrance? She willingly gave it a try. The strikers apparently thought she was simply out for a horseback ride or making house calls. They let her through the picket line. What they didn't know was that the payroll was hidden on her person. The workers were paid, and the strike was over.

The grateful mine owner invited her to a fancy dinner party at his home, along with all the other principals and management. He told her how much they appreciated her efforts. Laura, as a business owner herself, knew where her loyalties were. Superintendents, speculators, owners, and men of influence were lucrative clientele. Besides a great dinner and accolades, Laura received healthy tips. Her deceit didn't endear her to the working men in town, but she thought it was time to move on anyway. She wanted to work in a smaller town. (At one time, Leadville was the second-largest city in Colorado.) Some of her friends were sad to see her go. They gave her a suitcase stuffed with champagne, some of which she reportedly drank with the train crew. According to certain legends, she shared the rest of the case with law officers in Salida, her destination, to gain their goodwill.

Laura thought Salida was a good move. It was a stop on the Denver & Rio Grande Railway in central Colorado, about seventy miles southwest of Colorado Springs. Compared to Leadville, Salida felt smaller and less frenetic. By 1900, she opened her own place on Front Street. She was near the Denver & Rio Grande station, which had a healthy population of men. She expanded; in 1904, Laura built cottages and remodeled. For the first time in many years, she felt as if she had a home. But even after settling in, she didn't stop drinking, though she apparently reduced her intake somewhat. One of her employees who'd been with her for years said she saw Laura sloppy drunk only several times, which was a departure from her binge days.

Ironically for one who'd been hard to tame, Laura expected her girls to follow a certain code of behavior. They were expected to be well-dressed, kempt, and nicely mannered—and to wear the latest styles. "Madam Laura," one of her boarders recounted years later, "never wanted us girls to talk loud; we was always taught to watch our language. We parlor girls never used four-letter words." Laura taught them, "You can still be a lady." She rarely lost her temper, but her workers were expected to keep their rooms neat and living spaces tidy, which Laura believed infused a sense of dignity. One of her boarders described how Laura did business. She'd call upstairs and tell her ladies that gentlemen were in the parlor:

Laura's parlor house on Front Street in Salida was conveniently near the railroad station. She also owned cribs across the street. PHOTOGRAPH COURTESY OF DENVER PUBLIC LIBRARY SPECIAL COLLECTIONS, DPL X-13361.

> We'd never go over and sit next to a new man in town. We'd sit across the room on the divan or on chairs. Or we might sit in a nice pose on the library table. In the parlor—where the callers were always referred to as gentlemen—they would always sit down and talk awhile, while the girls remained at another part of the room. Then a man might say to one of the girls, "Why don't you come over here and sit down and talk to me." But even after accepting his invitation, and sitting down next to him, we would still behave like refined ladies. We would make no play for him, such as touching him or patting him, or any of that stuff, but would always talk to him the way Miss Laura wanted us to, when she used the words courteously and nicely. Then after a while he'd usually say "Let's go upstairs." (from Max Miller and Fred M. Mazzulla, *Holladay Street*, Ballantine Books, 1962)

The caricature of Laura as a wild thing makes a good story—and part of the fabrication might have happened, at least on some level. For a businesswoman, the bravado was good press. But there was another side of Laura that is less well known but no less interesting.

We're fortunate that, in the early 1950s (during the last few years of her life), Laura Evens sat for a series of revealing interviews, recorded on tape and transcribed. The old woman had an opportunity to tell her story. The interviews are revealing and candid—with some parts likely more story than fact. Still, she's one of the few women in her profession who had this opportunity. As an added bonus, we're also fortunate that some of her friends, people who knew her well, were also interviewed. We still aren't sure when Laura was born; she was purposefully elusive about the date. But we do get a wider view of the girl, the woman, and the madam.

Laura was a gambler who especially loved card games. It's also obvious that she loved a dare, and (as we'll see) few things were more enticing to her than a good bet. She was funny and charming, referring to herself in a self-deprecating manner as a racehorse in a jackass stall. As an old lady, she still lied about her age with a gleam in her eye. She could be a little loud and slightly vulgar but always commanding. Even in the last years of her life, she was articulate. Her interviewer commented that he could find only one inconsistency in their hours of conversation: Laura's hedging about her age. She was proud of her literacy and never failed to point out her colleagues who couldn't read (the famous Denver madam Jennie Rogers, for example).

The interviews give us a first hand glimpse of a dynamic woman, something missing from our other madam profiles. Her sketches and anecdotes about Colorado boomtowns are wonderful. Sometimes, her local color feels as tight as an unpolished Mark Twain vignette. Her "rolling" storytelling style, ear for dialogue, and gift for the oral tradition have provided us with a slice of life that makes us feel like we were there. Laura made no apologies for her hyperbole and, like Twain, often told her stories in a deadpan fashion, hiding the nub in the narrative. She also liked to point out that Mattie Silks and Jennie Rogers and their houses were filled with old, over-the-hill women.

Laura told her story and responded to questions in the interviews in the way she thought they *ought* to be told, and the truth would not get in her way. She could be harsh, petty, or kind. Notice her voice in the following excerpt. It tells us about her personality. Built like a dramatic monologue or a slam poem, Laura's description of Maxie (the working girl who rented a crib across the street from her brothel), while less than kind, truly needs to be read aloud so you can hear and feel Laura's voice. Maxie, by the way, was the first of four wives of Jack Dempsey, the famed prizefighter. It's obvious that Laura didn't approve of Maxie or her indifferently colored hair, but she was fond of Jack and knew him personally. The following is from Reel #8, November 8, 1952, collected by Fred M. Mazzulla. The punctuation here has been cleaned up and extraneous words omitted. You can almost picture Laura on a stage, presenting it at a storytelling festival. This is the real Laura:

> Well, she [Maxie] wasn't a pretty woman. She wasn't so red-haired . . . but she was stylish, haven't you seen women . . . no matter [what] you put on them . . . they look classy? She was a likable sort of devil, oh such a drunkard. One day I looked across the street and there was a procession. [She was] lying on her back, curtains all up . . . the bright lights on . . . stripped stark naked . . . well, I couldn't put up with that . . . because I always tried to run a first-class place. That kind of foolishness . . . that was galling. That is as bad as this nudist colony you got down in Denver . . . isn't that awful. Then they close a first-class sporting house . . . and allow that.

Laura was a "teller" at heart. Her witticisms were loaded with bits of social commentary that were both precise and ambiguous. Her stories poked fun at the men and women who needed to buy or sell favors on every level. We learn more about her in the following description, which is also from Reel #8. Even though she was middle-aged when this incident took place, Laura's lifelong sense of recklessness and passion remain audible. We also see Laura as a mythological trickster, a woman who lived on the edge of traditional morality—the kind of person who wanders back and forth over an imaginary line and is doomed to fit in neither world. She manipulated this bumbling lawman, Ike Howe, whenever she could, but more importantly, we see her discuss her lifelong love of horses:

> I was always . . . damn foolishness. [I was] racing up and down main street . . . a preacher on one side . . . and one of the officials . . . on the other . . . . [H]e would turn the corner . . . my horse . . . upsets him . . . the priest runs up on another woman's porch with his little rubber-tired rig . . . knocks down the porch.
>
> I used to race all the time. Old Ike Howe was the marshal. "Laura, what do you mean coming down Main Street," . . . he says. "I got to arrest you." . . . I said "I'll bet you ten dollars you can't drive that horse to the barn. . . . [Y]ou just [have] to go up the corner over this way." . . . [R]ight across the street from the Sherman was all the livery stables.
>
> Oh my God, she [her mare, Johnny] took him around that corner . . . . [Y]ou know I taught her if I wanted her to stop, she just stopped like that . . . when [the marshal] ran into the leaves hollering whoa . . . whoa . . . well . . . how could he control her . . . she threw him over the dashboard.
>
> He said, "I'm going to forbid you driving that horse." I said, "You try." Oh, the automobiles come and I sold her. I tell you it broke my heart. I worshipped her. I was crazy about that horse.

Laura loved all things equine and claimed to be a good rider. Sid Jennowitz, an old-timer from Leadville, talked about how Laura would get up at dawn and ride in the mountains. She liked to rent a tall, red horse and rode sidesaddle on the trails. On one occasion, Laura went on a hunting and fishing trip with her friends. Apparently, the party hadn't planned well, or the fish weren't biting and big game was scarce. They were running out of food, so one of the men killed a large rattlesnake. He cut it up and told them it was fish. Laura said nothing ever tasted so good.

Laura had a soft spot for her animals, but sadly her relationship with her daughter was strained. Laura was a detached mother at best, and Lucille could never quite forgive her for abandoning her family. In 1940, Lucille distributed a "defamatory circular" that led the FBI to investigate some of her mother's business practices and associates, though no charges were brought.

Dogs and cats, on the other hand, don't care if you're a whore who's made a lot of mistakes. Fellow madam and good friend Lillian Powers gave Laura a black and tan dog that liked to sleep near the foot of Laura's bed. They became fast friends, and she called him Mr. Pimp. The faithful dog took care of Laura and was a good companion. Occasionally, he'd growl at someone he didn't like. He lived to be fourteen years old. When he was ailing, she gently put him in a nearby chair and covered him with a blanket so he wouldn't get cold. He died peacefully while she was playing cards. She also had cats, but there was one particular black feline that was special. When this cat was about to have kittens, Laura put her on a bed so she'd be comfortable during the travail. Laura was the godmother of the kittens, playing with them as they grew. She also had ducks, turkeys, and rabbits in her menagerie, as well as a pet donkey that she liked to ride.

Another pet was an old milk cow that Laura befriended somewhere. The cow liked to hang around the brothel in Salida like any other pet. She was lovable, but like most cows, she wasn't too bright. One day, the cow walked onto the wooden cellar doors near the house. The doors collapsed, as the creature weighed about 1,700 pounds, and she fell into a coal storage area. Luckily, she was unhurt, but Laura had to hire several workmen with a good-sized hoist and sling to extract the bovine from the cellar. It was an expensive rescue.

Laura also had several pigs that took a special fancy to her because she gave them snacks. They followed her like dogs, presumably hoping for a treat. One day, she walked to the bank and the pigs tagged along. After she finished her transaction and returned home, a banker called to tell her that the pigs were still at the bank and she needed to come get them.

In 1918, the Spanish flu hit Colorado. The first to die was a student in Denver, and the virus spread quickly. Schools, churches, theaters, and other public gathering areas were closed—even the lobbies of post offices. Fever, fatigue, and headaches were the first signs. Then came coughing so violent it could injure stomach muscles and cause the victim to cough up foamy blood. Death could occur within hours. Salida was quarantined. Guards allowed no one in or out of town. Parlor houses were closed, but some of the cribs, which were private residences, remained in business. The number of sick taxed the medical facilities of the town. A doctor asked Laura if any of her "girls" could help with nursing. They converted the St. Clair Hotel into a hospital and did their part, including nursing the doctor's family, all of whom were ill. The Reverend Oakley, head of a league aimed at closing down the red-light districts, had previously been quite outspoken against local madams, naming Laura Evens in particular. Laura found it amusing that one of her soiled doves nursed him and his family when they had the flu. She said he didn't change his mind about the evils of prostitution, but he was grateful for the Christian help and was no longer as adamant. In fact, he wanted to hire the woman who had helped his family as a companion for his wife and a housekeeper. She returned instead to the brothel.

Fred Mazzulla also interviewed Fern Pedro, one of the women who worked for Laura. Fern talked about going into the business at sixteen and how she ran around with a bunch of wild girls. She got married, ran away, and was lost to her family. In Pueblo, Colorado, she heard about Laura and went to apply for a job. Fern said that the old madam tried hard to talk her out of entering the profession.

Madam Laura stayed in business for a long time. Officially, the town council shut her house down in 1950. Then she rented rooms. She died on April 4, 1953. If the birth date we have is correct, she would have been seventy-nine years old.

Beat Up by the Press,

Men, and Other Working Ladies

IN THE 1800S, THE PENALTIES FOR BEATING A DOG and beating a prostitute were about the same. If a girl's face was bruised too badly, she probably couldn't work until it cleared up. And since she had no rights because she was a whore, if she was raped, as sometimes happened, there was little or no recourse with the law. The prevailing notion was: how can you rape a whore or a common woman? If she wanted justice, she'd have to take the law into her own hands, which some occasionally did.

If there was an incident or altercation involving a working woman, her name was dragged through the newspaper. Yet every effort was made to protect the man who was caught, if you'll excuse the pun, with his pants down. A typical article in the County Herald from Boulder, Colorado, for example, read that lawmen "arrested X and Y" to protect the men's names and reputations. The article then gave all the details about the girls involved, listing names, addresses, past offenses, and whatever else they could drag up. It's easy to see why most prostitutes used pseudonyms to protect their families in the event of arrest.

Women certainly feared physical abuse from clients, but there was another danger: fellow prostitutes. Painted women often fought among themselves, and it could be more than hair pulling. Girls from rival pleasure studios feuded with each other in what often was essentially a turf war. Sometimes these confrontations led to fisticuffs, but they could be as innocent as practical jokes. In one town, a house had been in business for quite some time until an enterprising madam fired up her own red light about a block away. The new competition started to steal customers. There were harsh words as each house vied for clients. One day, the girls from the older business tried to get even by nailing the door shut on one of the newer doves as she visited the outhouse, but not before throwing in a hornet's nest to keep the poor girl company. The girl in the outhouse had a number of welts from the stings and couldn't work for a few days. Since her competitors were on a roll with the outhouse, they went further, sneaking into the backyard to put itching powder on bedclothes that were drying on the line. Later, neighbors could hear foul words a block away as the girls discovered the mischief and started scratching. After several days, the tricksters wondered why men were walking up to their house but then turning away. After a few days of no business and no income, they discovered that there was a measles quarantine sign on their front door.

Sisters and madams aside, clients were still the biggest danger. A prostitute never knew if her next trick was going to beat her up. Few prostitutes could say they'd never been physically abused by a client. The fact that they could do little about it was a given. They had mostly lost their rights to use the legal system when they joined the sisterhood.

9

Pearl DeVere

The Fated Madam of Cripple Creek and Her Last Rejection

On July 5, 1897, Madam Pearl DeVere died at thirty-six years old from a morphine overdose after a long evening of drinking alcohol. But was it accidental or was it suicide?

When Maud Stone noticed that Pearl's breathing appeared abnormal and her skin was pale, she summoned Dr. Hereford. He could not awaken Pearl. At 3:30 P.M., she was pronounced dead—just six months after opening the Old Homestead, one of the most talked-about brothels in the West. The previous evening, July 4, Pearl had thrown a "party to end all parties." It was a lavish affair; no expense was spared. She intended it to be the grandest celebration of her career, and it was. Tragically, it was also her last.

For the party, Pearl wore an exquisite and expensive pink chiffon gown graced with seed pearls and sequins. Worth $800, it had been made in Paris. As the queen of her ball, she glided from guest to guest, making sure everything was perfect. There were exotic flowers, cases of vintage champagne, Russian caviar, fine food, and two orchestras, with dancing, gambling, and—of course—beautiful women, most in their early twenties.

> *Soirees were common at finer parlor houses, but not on this level. It was not only a way to advertise and show off her girls, it was also a belated grand opening of the Old Homestead. Her guest list was exclusive. You had to have a financial pedigree to make the cut.*
>
> *Pearl catered exclusively to the wealthy. Cripple Creek had more than its share of well-heeled gentlemen. A night with one of her girls could cost between $250 and $300, a small fortune at a time when the average working man earned $3 a day. Reservations were always required. The house had Old World charm: wallpaper imported from France and brass fixtures from London. It also had the latest modern conveniences: phonograph, intercom, telephone, and bathrooms.*

Pearl DeVere was at the top of her profession. She was heavily in debt and felt financial pressure to make her business work, but the party was a promising start. Arranging an event like this was stressful, as there were so many last-minute details. Some of her associates commented after her death that she was edgy, nervous, and hadn't had enough sleep, but butterflies before a big launch are normal. A newspaper account hinted that sometime during or after the party she may have had an argument with "a gentleman from Denver," possibly someone special, maybe even the man who had given her the imported gown. The paper also implied that Pearl had hinted that the mysterious gentleman was leaving his wife. Such tempestuous circumstances might have been amusing to her if the outcome hadn't been so final. She would have enjoyed the fanfare, as publicity was good in her line of work. She was said to be a trim, orderly woman—handsome if not beautiful. Unfortunately, no photographs of her have survived.

Pearl DeVere (sometimes spelled de Vere) wasn't her real name, nor even her first professional name. We don't know her real name, but we do know that the famous madam was born in the Midwest (maybe Chicago) and raised around Evansville, Indiana. Something unfortunate must have derailed her life, because she was working the mean streets of Denver by the age that most girls nowadays get their learner's permit to drive. At the time of her death, she'd been out of her family's home for twenty years.

Any details of her young professional life are similarly murky. No one worried about a teenaged prostitute's curriculum vitae. She survived, which means she was lucky and smart. Pearl also was personable and clever, and she intuitively knew how to take care of herself and move up in the underworld. She ran with a shady crowd but proved she was ambitious and streetwise. She began using the name Mrs. Isabel Martin. She was regularly seen with a gambler named Martin, but they weren't officially married. The title at least gave her a pretense of respectability when they traveled.

Pearl—or Mrs. Martin—accompanied Mr. Martin on a series of fairy-tale adventures. Having survived the streets, she lived high and fast. It appears Martin was a good gambler, and Pearl developed a taste for the finer things and honed her courtesan crafts. The couple apparently traveled internationally. Legends have Pearl carefully studying the best brothels in Paris and taking mental notes. She appreciated their opulence, but she was a serious student of the business side of the exclusive bawdy profession. She paid attention to the furnishings and the floor plans.

A gambler's life is feast or famine, and this understandably might have grown tiresome for Pearl. At some point, the couple had a falling-out. A simple, unstable plotline is all we know; we can't vouch for the authenticity, but it's a good story. Let's take a dramatic pause and listen for the drumroll. They argued and parted. Surely such quarreling had happened before. The ever-romantic Martin—the suave, globe-trotting gambler—beat lady luck and broke the bank (won all the money) at the roulette wheel in one of Europe's finest casinos. Considering that he started at odds of thirty-seven to one, simply breaking even against the house edge was notable. As he was cashing in his untold fortune, he received a note from Pearl. It said she didn't care for him any longer. Heartbroken, Martin took out his pistol, made some clever quip, and blew his brains out all over the roulette wheel. The unsinkable Pearl went back to Denver to regroup. Maybe she would've stayed with him longer if she'd known he'd beat the odds.

You can't buy this kind of publicity. She was now, literally, a woman to die for. Rumors followed her and added to her courtesan intrigue. She had enough money to start anew. During the Panic of 1893, great fortunes were lost. Silver mining was officially declared dead when the U.S. government repealed the Sherman Silver Act, which had effectively subsidized silver mining. Business was suffering, but Pearl came up with a plan.

It started with the headlines. A rancher named Bob Womack showed up at the assay office in Colorado Springs, triggering a whole new front: the Cripple Creek Gold Rush. His cry was heard around the world. It caused a landslide that uprooted tens of thousands of men from their homes with the promise of amazing wealth. Thirty-one-year-old Pearl would get her share. The mining district was only 125 miles away; location was everything. And as it turned out, the promises of fortunes weren't exaggerated. The district would produce nearly 24 million ounces of gold (at today's prices, this would be worth around $40 billion). Located in a mountainous valley, it was fifty miles south of Pikes Peak. Winfield Scott Stratton, a former carpenter, was the first millionaire with gold banked from his Independence Mine in Cripple Creek. Other fantasy fortune stories about sudden millionaires flooded the news: James Burns, a gas fitter; R. McKinnie, a laborer; John Harnan, a laborer; E. M. Veigne, a teacher; and so on.

The Womack family had ranched in the area since 1876. A cow had broken her leg in a clear steam called Cripple Creek, and the name caught on. Bob Womack loved ranching, but he never kicked gold fever. When he wasn't working cattle, he prospected. He found color in the creek but wandered the canyons for twelve years trying to unravel the geologic puzzle. Certain he'd found the mother lode above Poverty Gulch, he filed a claim called the El Paso Load. Bob liked his whiskey, and he needed some money. He didn't know how to work his claim. One night, after several glasses of whiskey, he sold it for $500 to a smooth-talking fellow. The buyer went on to form the Cripple Creek Mining District. Bob died broke.

Pearl procured a tidy framed house on Myers Avenue and was successful immediately. In Cripple Creek, she started using the name we know her by, Pearl DeVere. She thought it gave her a hint of mystery.

She liked pearls, so the first name, Pearl, was easy. She might have borrowed her last name from a local clairvoyant named DeVere. Apparently, this woman had a crystal ball, and she told fortunes and divined the location of gold mines. At any rate, the name sounded French and had an air of intrigue. In 1895, Pearl married Charles B. Flynn. This was a surprising move, according to local gossip. Flynn was a successful but small businessman who ran a mill. He seemed steady, and she undoubtedly thought he would be successful. Each worked at their trades and prospered respectably for a time.

Then their dreams quite literally went up in smoke. The couple lost everything in what were referred to as the Cripple Creek Fires of 1896. Most of the town was destroyed. At least six people died, and others were injured. Estimates vary, but damages could've been between $1.5 and $2 million (about $60 million today). Thousands were left homeless. (The weather at 9,400 feet was chilly, but survivors reasoned that summer was just around the corner.) Fire was a real danger, and mining towns were especially vulnerable. Buildings were constructed quickly and cheaply, which usually meant wooden frames and siding. A miner's plan was to cash out with big profits as soon as possible. In the first wave, nothing was built to last, as mines could play out fast.

The first fire alarm rang on Saturday, April 25, 1896, just before noon. A fire had broken out on Myers Avenue in a room above the Central Dance Hall, where Jennie Laurel and her "date" were arguing over money. The discussion turned ugly, and Jennie started to take punches and blows. At some point, she fell, overturning a stove and spilling its fuel. Flames quickly consumed the room, and the discussion was over. The two fled in a panic, as did others. In minutes, the building was gone. The afternoon wind, typical in springtime, picked up, and before long the north side of the street was ablaze. The fire spread into a residential area, destroying homes. Some buildings were blown apart with dynamite in an effort to corral the devastation by eliminating fuel for the fire. It didn't work. The fire became so hot that firemen couldn't get close enough to use their hoses. Fortunately, some of the businesspeople and residents had enough time to get out alive; some even salvaged a few items. Prisoners were let out of the jail before the newly constructed building burned. When the wind subsided, firemen managed to get the fire under control after midnight.

The second fire bell rang on Wednesday, April 29, at 1:30 P.M. A fire again broke out on Myers Avenue in a section that had already been mostly destroyed. Betsy Kelly, a waitress, discovered a grease fire in the kitchen of the Portland Hotel. The building was quickly consumed, and the fire spread to Bennett Avenue. The structures west of Third Street were destroyed. Ammunition and gunpowder at Wright Hardware Store fueled a spectacular explosion.

Confusion reigned on Bennett Avenue as fire consumed blocks of Cripple Creek's wooden buildings. PHOTOGRAPH BY EDGAR A. YELTON, COURTESY OF THE DENVER PUBLIC LIBRARY WESTERN HISTORY COLLECTION, X-868.

Thousands were homeless. Stunned, the townsfolk saw their worst fears realized. Pearl and Charles watched and helped as they could. But the strain of this loss would prove too much for their marital relationship. Pearl was determined to rebuild, but Charles decided that he'd had enough. Being married to a madam was a high-maintenance relationship on the best of days. Discouraged and flat broke, he was wiped out. Charles took a job in Mexico. Neither seemed to be distraught that their relationship had gone cold as quickly as the fire's ashes.

As it turned out, Pearl was bankable. As if she had been preparing for this moment, she launched into planning and construction, doing business on the side. She may have had time to grab a few valuables

As flames roared and smoke billowed above Cripple Creek on April 29, 1896, men dynamited buildings between Myers and Bennett Avenues in a futile attempt to stop the fire. PHOTOGRAPH BY EDGAR A. YELTON, COURTESY OF THE DENVER PUBLIC LIBRARY WESTERN HISTORY COLLECTION, X-869.

before the blaze; most working women had an emergency stash, never knowing when they might have to leave suddenly. She was able to secure several loans, including one from New York. This time, she would construct her dream brothel of brick, not easily burned wood. She built on the same location and called it the Old Homestead. The details were consuming, but she was up to the task and watched over its construction: elaborate lights, hand-painted wallpaper, running water, bathtubs, hand-blown chandeliers, custom hardwood gaming tables, silk screens, a wine room, lace, and other finery. Pearl's private room was upstairs at the end of the hall. The place still stands today. (If you're ever in the Cripple Creek Mining District, visit the Old Homestead. You can't miss it since it's the only remaining "brothel building" in town. It's now a museum, located at 353 Myers, a block east of Bennett Avenue. It's open seasonally, so check its webpage. The tours are family-friendly and delightful. Nearby in Victor, you can book a tour of the mine.)

Like other madams, Pearl knew the importance of advertising. In that era, there were red and blue, pocket-sized books printed on cheap paper that advertised bars, dance halls, and brothels. These books were available in rail stations, saloons, barbershops, and other

DeVere's Old Homestead, now a museum, was luxurious for its time and place. PHOTOGRAPH BY BILL PEERY, COURTESY OF DENVER PUBLIC LIBRARY SPECIAL COLLECTIONS X-751.

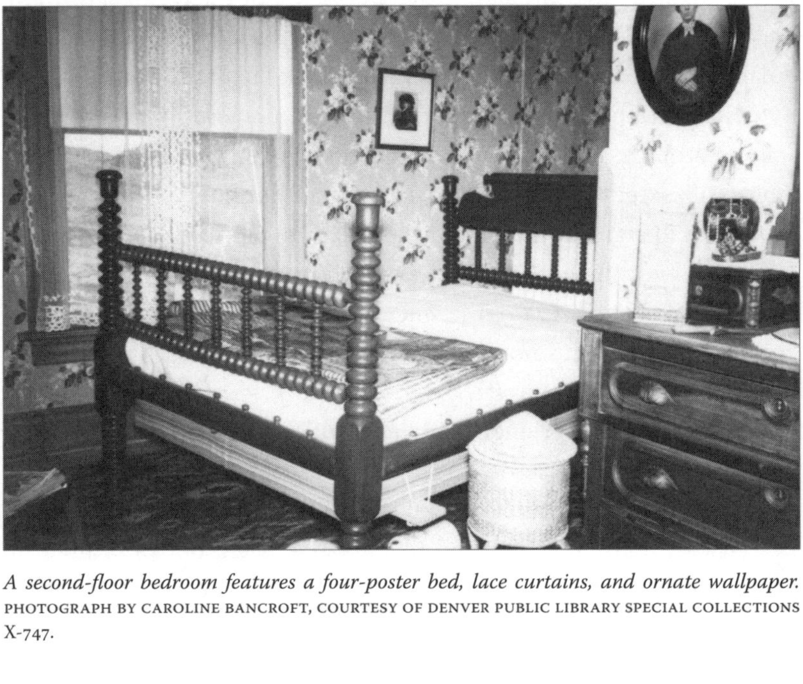

A second-floor bedroom features a four-poster bed, lace curtains, and ornate wallpaper. PHOTOGRAPH BY CAROLINE BANCROFT, COURTESY OF DENVER PUBLIC LIBRARY SPECIAL COLLECTIONS X-747.

locations. Madams also took afternoon rides that served as another form of advertisement. Pearl enjoyed going for rides in her carriage. She liked horses and the afternoon air on her face, but mostly this ritual was good for business. She always wore different, fancy clothes—much to the envy, it was said, of some of the local women. Sometimes she'd take one of her girls with her—especially if the girl was new to the area. She liked to rent a pair of powerful black horses and drive far too fast. Other times, Pearl rode sidesaddle, as a proper lady did. Part of the Pearl mythology has her wearing a derby hat.

As the manager of an expensive house of sin, she expected her girls to be well dressed and refined. It wasn't unusual for a madam like Pearl to coach her employees in the finer things. Such schooling could include a crash course in manners, snippets of French, music and vocal lessons, literature, and the arts. While she took 60 percent of each girl's earnings, Pearl and her ladies had disposable income, and local merchants welcomed their money. Many working women used shopping trips to advertise, shock, or embarrass local women. Children weren't allowed on Myers Avenue, but they still could see too much at a general store on Bennett Avenue. After the town settled, the girls were less welcome in public.

Parlor girls were supposed to have more refined behavior than brazen streetwalkers and common bawdy women; the latter could be offensive and vulgar. When respectable women complained, their voices were heard. Being in public was a problem as the town settled down and tried to put on a semblance of respectability. Sheriff Wilson regulated business hours to appease both sides. In Cripple Creek, working women were allowed to shop when stores weren't busy in the mornings or afternoons—out of sight, out of mind. Such ordinances increased social isolation but were expected. So was an increase in the sin tax: madams had to pay $16 a month, while each girl paid $6.

The Old Homestead was built quickly and soon opened. There was money to be made. Certainly, there were some last details to address, but men with money couldn't be put off. Six months after the red light was turned on, the grand opening was scheduled. Engraved invitations were sent out; Fourth of July 1897 would be the biggest party in the city's history. Thirty-six-year-old Pearl seemed to have it all: the best house not only in town but in the Rocky Mountains. Nothing was left to chance. She was proud of her outlandishly expensive gown, which cost more than some men made in a year. She knew people were talking about her dress. It was part of the personal brand she was trying to convey. Of course, she wore pearls—her working namesake. The house was packed, food was superb, wine flowed, men danced and gambled, and musicians played late into the night. By all appearances, the evening was going well. And then it all went wrong. Pearl surely died by her own hand, but evidence points to an accidental overdose. Perhaps she was stressed or edgy. She may have had a disagreement with a man she possibly cared for or felt let down after the evening was over. None of this necessarily made her suicidal. It's not accurate, either, to make comparisons with Ella Wellington's dramatic exit. There were too many differences. Let's take a closer look.

Pearl had been drinking that evening, probably too much. The party was over by dawn, so she tried to sleep. We can agree that she was worn down, fatigued, and in a fragile state. Indeed, she *might* have been using morphine regularly and perhaps was feeling symptoms of withdrawal: anxiety, nervousness, depression, and agitation. She might have used cocaine to boost her energy during the day, since a lot was riding on this venture. We don't know for sure. Drugs were a crutch widely used by prostitutes, and madams weren't exempt. Sadly, it was a way of life and one of the artifacts of her trade, along with perfume, makeup, and mail-order venereal disease cures. Taking morphine-based sleep aids wouldn't turn an eye; they were almost as common as aspirin or acetaminophen today. We know that, on the evening in question, Pearl drank a lot and overdosed on morphine.

There were no so-called street drugs or "Schedule I or II" pharmaceuticals. Everything was sold over the counter. In the nineteenth century, opium, morphine, and cocaine were the central ingredients in many everyday medicines. They were used widely, considered innocuous, and prescribed for headaches, hay fever, crying babies, cough, toothaches, arthritis—really any ailment. For example, one popular product advertised in many magazines was Mrs. Winslow's Soothing Syrup, marketed to young mothers. It was designed to help get those rowdy youngsters to sleep. It was a morphine- and alcohol-based syrup. In a few years, it would rightly be called a "baby killer" and taken off the market.

Morphine (a derivative of opium) was widely used during the Civil War. Doctors saw its pain-killing abilities as nothing less than miraculous and used it liberally to help Union and Confederate soldiers alike cope with gruesome wounds and often equally gruesome surgeries, including amputation. But the addictive nature of morphine was not really understood. Consequently, in the aftermath of the war, there were tens of thousands of morphine addicts in the United States, many of them former soldiers. Alcohol use was also widespread, and drinking often went hand in hand with morphine use. (Matters did not improve with the synthesis and commercialization in the 1890s of a new opiate, heroin, marketed by the Bayer drug company as a "non-addictive" alternative to morphine. In fact, heroin proved to be even more addictive and lethal.)

Opiates and alcohol are both depressants that slow breathing and heart rate, and frequent use tends to build tolerance so that over time, the user must increase the dose to get the same high. The consequences can be deadly.

We know that Madam Pearl was rundown, likely feeling a bit out of sorts, and needing sleep—but not the "big sleep." Through her habit, she had likely built a tolerance for morphine, so she needed more to achieve the same effect. This was the tricky part. Perhaps, under pressure, she miscalculated. Even intelligent people like Pearl were vulnerable. At any rate, the combination of morphine and alcohol impeded her judgment and then hit her with a respiratory and cardiac double whammy.

Maud Stone checked on her that morning and knew immediately that there was a serious problem. You don't work at a whorehouse, even a high-end one, and not instantly recognize the telltale signs of an opiate overdose. The drug affects the central nervous system, and the first giveaway is that breathing becomes slow and raspy. Maud tried to wake Pearl, to no avail. Pearl's skin would've been clammy and her body limp. Her lips and fingers might have been blue. It took Maud about three seconds to call for help. The doctor tried but couldn't bring her out of her coma. He laid her on her side so she wouldn't choke and used all the other tricks he knew. But Pearl's heart and breathing stopped, and he pronounced her dead. Dr. Hereford labeled it an accidental overdose. The *Cripple Creek Times* also suggested that her death was accidental: "No evidence the death was intentional." However, there was—and still is—a lot of speculation.

The final rejection by her family after her passing was sadly predictable, but it illustrated a harsh social reality. It's normal that she wanted her family to think well of her. We don't know if Pearl had been home to Indiana to visit her family for some time, but it's obvious there was some contact. Her mother and sister assumed she was a successful dress designer who worked for the well-to-do women of Cripple Creek. She told her people she owned a business, DeVere Gowns.

It gets a little confusing at this point. Apparently, someone contacted her family about her death. The funeral home, Fairley Bros. and Lampman, received a wire from her family telling the directors to embalm her body. Apparently, her brother-in-law said in the telegram that someone would come to Colorado and bring her body back to Evansville, Indiana, for burial. Sometime later, Pearl's sister showed up in Cripple Creek.

There are hints that her family was financially comfortable and perhaps socially prominent. They were religious people, deeply rooted in their respectability. Coming to get her body and bring it home would've been costly, so that suggested that the family was solvent. Pearl's sister's shock when she saw the "dead woman" at the funeral home is telling; the poor woman's emotions evolved from grief to anger, from shame to rage. Certainly there was some mistake, as the woman with the dyed red hair in the French gown looked like a whore. The shock of her sister's death was replaced by a much harsher realization—the cruelest cut of all: the horror of what her fallen sister really did for a living. Pearl had sold her soul for thirty pieces of silver. Her sister gave the funeral director and anyone else she could find an earful. They had wasted her time and money. In a fit of righteous indignation, she suggested that the sheriff burn Pearl's possessions, because her family didn't want anything to do with the dead woman. She was disgraced. The sister got on the next train. Even when you're dead, if you're fallen, you almost never get to go home again.

The fact that she didn't have enough money for her own burial confirms that Pearl lived well beyond her means; her expensive lifestyle was mortgaged to the hilt of her colored hair. The funeral cost about $200, and there were other unsettled bills. Nothing could be done until the estate was probated—and that would take time. Johnny Nolan, who ran Johnny Nolan's Saloon, put Pearl's things up for auction to pay for the undertakers and funeral. Then an anonymous envelope arrived from Denver with $1,000 to cover her burial and some immediate bills. The town was offended by her sister's callous rejection and did what they could. In response, the *Cripple Creek Times* editorialized and said, "Cripple Creek can bury its own dead."

There were carriages and businessmen and ladies from the row lined up to pay their respects. Pearl had a great send-off. The Elks Lodge band marched in procession, and law enforcement officials paraded on horseback. To show they took care of their own, they buried Pearl in consecrated ground on Mount Pisgah (where, just the previous year, mining investors Horace Bennett and Julius Myers had donated forty acres for a cemetery), just like respectable folks. Legend has it that the band played the famous song "There'll Be a Hot Time in the Old Town Tonight." They say it was a reference to Myers Avenue—the street of sin—in Cripple Creek.

Pearl got an official wooden marker. Her name was mentioned in a 1929 silent film—*The Shady Lady*—but she was nearly forgotten by the 1930s. The Old Homestead continued as a brothel under different owners for several more decades. They say someone called her husband, Charles Flynn, to tell him of her passing. There was no response.

The Culture of True Womanhood

(or the Cult of Domesticity)

WOMEN WHO ATTACKED VICE in the nineteenth century were the great-grandmothers of modern women's movements. In the nineteenth century, a "Culture of True Womanhood"—later shortened in the 1960s to the "Cult of True Womanhood" and also called the "Cult of Domesticity"—defined most women's roles in society and at home. A true woman adhered to a value system or an ideal code of behavior, centered on home and husband, on domestic activity. The woman was the moral compass of her home. According to this belief system, a woman, by nature and design, was dependent upon her man because she was naturally frail. She was inclined toward feminine things: tending flowers, raising children, and doing housework—woman's work. Mentally, she was weak and inferior to men; thus, she should avoid literature and focus only on the Bible or religious stories, because intellectual endeavors might cause hysteria. A true woman:

- *was pure and chaste. This was black and white; she was either good or bad.*
- *knew her place was in the home. Working outside the home was expected only of men.*
- *was submissive to a man, by God's decree and the natural order of the universe.*
- *wasn't interested in delving into heady, intellectual issues because she would lose her focus on home and duty—and it just wasn't good for her.*

As the nineteenth century progressed, these values persisted. Women gradually came to view themselves as the moral compass not only of the home but of society as a whole. Increasingly, they took up social causes, leading to the "moral purity" or "social purity" movements. (The word social was a euphemism for "sexual," i.e., social disease for venereal disease.) Women were in the vanguard of abolishing prostitution because they felt responsible for cleaning up their towns and making them safe for families and children. As families began to replace the wilder elements that had once dominated frontier towns, fewer nefarious businesses prospered and the social landscape evolved. Women started to see their towns and social issues in a different light. Prostitution, at one time almost a symbol of status for a frontier settlement, became a liability. Law and Order Leagues also tackled the vices of alcohol and gambling. By the latter part of the nineteenth century, moral abasement, venereal disease, and white slavery were also in the crosshairs. Crusaders, businessmen, government leaders, women's groups, concerned citizens, and suffragettes united under this common cause. Different groups went before Congress, arguing that prostitution and white slavery were social problems that had to be addressed. They also took aim at a number of other social issues (women's rights, low wages, and so on).

Sexual suppression was considered good manners for a proper human being. Specifically, if one were "refined," there should be little if any apparent interest in sexual behavior. A "proper" person, through abstinence and self-control, kept his or her self-respect and dignity. After all, man was just a little lower than the angels and needed to act like it. He wasn't an animal copulating indiscriminately in the bush. Only common folk (the ignorant) had large families, and only the vulgar and unconstrained would lower themselves by visiting lewd women.

Prostitution, therefore, became one of the great evils of the age. It debased the misguided men who sought the society of whores, along with the lowly, delinquent prostitutes (who were, in turn, victims of social inequality). Further, it debased womanhood in general. There was a special power in this movement. Women were able to take control and affect positive changes in this unique form of social Darwinism. It was a turf war, where people were literally taking back their neighborhoods, both morally and physically.

This change could only have occurred because of the dynamic evolution of society's view of women, thanks to the lingering remnants of chivalry and the "Cult of True Womanhood." An "ideal" woman was seen as a lovely, nearly asexual being, just slightly lower than the angels. (This was a radical step away from the Catholic and Calvinist dogma, which preached that women were naturally depraved and the cause of the Fall.) Thus, there was no place for prostitution. As Mary Murphy said in The Woman's West, *"Prostitution has no place within the ranks of true womanhood. They were 'public women,' belonging to all men, not one man, and therefore not quite woman at all."*

When a woman transgressed, she was censured, which helps explain why a common woman had so little respect. She was to be pitied (even if it was partially society's fault for providing so few opportunities); nevertheless, she had sold her God-given birthright.

This new moral mood reached a crescendo in England during August 1885 with the Labouchere Amendment (which lasted almost eighty years). Henry Labouchere proposed a law that he thought would be progressive, a law that would make "any act of gross indecency" a crime. The attorney general liked the law but suggested that anyone convicted of "gross indecency" should automatically be sentenced to two years of hard time. The law was strictly enforced. Occasionally, even celebrities were caught in its web. Oscar Wilde, the libertine playwright and novelist, got two years of hard labor after being convicted. One of the purposes of these acts was to protect women and children—and men—from "moral corruption." The framers of this law thought it would help prevent the debasing evil of prostitution, encourage women's rights, erase double standards, give women better educational opportunities, and create equal pay.

An important element of the movement was the women's clubs that began to spring up across the West. As June Croly wrote in History of the Woman's Club Movement in America, *"A wave of enthusiastic desire for social and mental improvement . . . [swept] through . . . small towns and remoter districts, . . . an intellectual crusade."*

After the Civil War, women were alarmed about loosening moral standards, which prompted them to gather into clubs. Many men had been away from home for quite some time during the war and were used to the rougher ways of army life. There was also a thriving trade in pornography. Men could easily purchase dirty pictures near army bases or at train stations, harbors, and docks. They could also order them through the mail. Add to this the number of risqué shows, which had formerly been underground but were now playing openly in theaters. The sight of women's legs and more incited even greater alarm.

By the middle of the nineteenth century, cartes de viste *(or dirty postcards) had become especially popular. One year in Great Britain, over 200 million pornographic postcards reportedly were printed. The photos ranged from a racy-looking woman on a couch showing stocking-clad legs to hardcore poses. The trade was so widespread that even the French poet Charles Baudelaire wrote a monogram about the dangers of pornography. This loosening of morals—while mild by contemporary standards—added fuel to the purity movement and became a topic of conversation for women's clubs. Anthony Comstock, a U.S. postal inspector, pushed for new federal obscenity laws. The Comstock or Parent Act was passed on March 3, 1873, making it illegal to circulate and trade articles of obscenity.*

"Vice societies" (part of the women's club movement) were established to fight moral corruption. By 1869, women were leading a fight to stop theatrical productions that showed women's legs. More formal women's organizations sprung up with a mandate to preserve morals and save the family unit. One of the strongest was the Woman's Christian Temperance Union (WCTU), which was founded in Ohio in 1874. Sixteen years later, sixty-three women's clubs founded the General Federation of Women's Clubs (GFWC), which peaked in the mid-1950s with a membership of nearly 900,000 women and 16,000 service clubs. Both of these organizations remain active today.

Daddy's in There---

And Our Shoes and Stockings and Clothes and Food Are in There, Too, and They'll Never Come Out.
—*Chicago American.*

WANTED--A FATHER; A LITTLE BOY'S PLEA

JULIA H. JOHNSON

A shy little boy stood peering
  Through the door of a bright saloon;
He looked as if food and clothing
  Would be thought a most welcome boon.

And one of the men, in passing,
  As if tossing a dog a bone,
Asked, "What do you want this evening?"
  In a rude and unkindly tone.

"I am wanting"—the boy's lips trembled—
  "I am wanting my father, sir."
And he gazed at the little tables
  Where the careless onlookers were.

It was there that he saw his father,
  But the man only shook his head,
And the boy, with his thin cheek burning,
  Ran away with a look of dread.

Oh, the fathers—the fathers wanted!
  How the heart-break, and bitter need,
With the longings, deep and piteous,
  For the wandering children plead.

May the children's call arouse them,
  May the fathers arise and go
With the young souls waiting for them,
  For the little ones need them so!

SERIES G. NO. 23.

The American Issue Publishing Co.,
Westerville Ohio

This temperance broadside published in 1917 shows destitute children waiting for their father outside a saloon. ILLUSTRATION COURTESY OF THE IIBRARY OF CONGRESS, LC-USZ62-54501.]

10

Lillian Powers

The Last of the Old West Madams

*T**HEY CALLED HER "TIGER LIL,"** although we're not sure how she came by that nickname. She was the last of the Colorado madams. She died quietly in her sleep in 1960. She said before she passed, "I have no regrets." Maybe so.*

Lillian worked Market Street in Denver before the turn of the century and knew Mattie Silks and Laura Evens personally. She also had a front-row seat in several of Colorado's boomtowns, so we have snapshots of the last days of the West thanks to several long interviews she gave before her passing.

Lillian insisted that being a common woman didn't mean you couldn't be neat and tidy. As a working girl, she fled Cripple Creek when a rival, "Leo the Lion," brandished a handgun; the drunken madam threatened to blow off Lillian's head and gave her that clichéd Old West ultimatum: "Be out of town by sundown." Lillian rightly feared for her life, because the whiskey-soaked Leo had a reputation for violence. Lillian packed her belongings and made the train, but not before she cleaned her cottage, leaving it spotless for the next renter. She had a simple rule: don't leave a mess for someone else to clean up.

Her fastidious and tidy behavior was also reflected in her bookkeeping and management skills. She paid attention to details and ran her "disorderly business" in an orderly fashion. Lillian said, "If you have a bunch of girls and don't make very much money, you're losing money." Tidy and careful with her earnings, she was able to live handsomely. As an old woman, careful not to leave any issues unresolved, she sold her properties, fixed her finances, and exited mortal life knowing that there'd be no financial messes for someone else to clean up.

She lived through two world wars, the development of the atomic bomb, and the glory days of the American West. What she thought of the election of John F. Kennedy, NASA, or the hit television show The Flintstones, *we can only wonder.*

Before she was Lillian Powers, her name was Minnie Mundsack. Born in 1873 in Wisconsin, she was a pretty farm girl who left home at sixteen to see the world. Although her family was poor, her parents saw to it that she learned to read and write—which was educated for a farm girl. She proved to be intelligent and witty, with a mind of her own. This no doubt troubled her poor mother, who was surely influenced by the thinking of her day. Society taught that, for women, it's better to pray than to think, and a woman's intellectual or material desires should never conflict with her domestic duties. The culture dictated that women were so sensitive and delicate that such endeavors would surely lead them away from God and their responsibilities.

The young Lillian respected how difficult and precarious life had been for her Scandinavian parents—immigrants hoping to carve out a living in a new land. The times were hard, and they struggled to keep food on the table. A new dress or a nice pair of shoes was a big deal because it took every penny to keep the farm going. Lillian knew her mother and father were living their dream and were willing to work themselves to death for it. It was how you paid the mortgage on the hope of a better life for your family, but it came with a high cost.

Maybe Lillian told herself that leaving meant one less mouth to feed. By the time she was a teenager, she was certain farm life wasn't what she wanted. Her mother labored seven days a week. She was up before first light, cooking, sewing, mending, gardening, tending babies, cleaning, washing—it never ended. Her mother looked older than she was. She never had time to sit down or socialize. The young girl wanted more—at least, she hoped for more. Lillian was secretly pleased that, as she aged, she looked younger than she was.

There was a wide world beyond the green farmland of the Midwest. She'd read stories, romances, and fairy tales. She'd seen new clothes and fancy things in the shops that she could never have, could never even touch. She must have wondered about corsets and how a fashionable woman in her day might wear twenty or thirty pounds of clothing. Perhaps she was not yet aware of the Victorian notion that young women could be ruined by reading, particularly novels.

Lillian especially liked dainty pillows and other pretty things that would seem out of place in her mother's house, things that were impractical and expensive when you had to buy flour for bread and seeds for planting. Later, even in her crib days, Lillian would have what she called "dainty" things to make her environment more livable and genteel. Lillian also had a secret dream that seemed far-fetched to her parents, simple folks from the old country who could never see past their farm. She wanted to experience, firsthand, the Wild West before it was gone. Backbreaking toil wasn't her dream. She was willing to work, but she hoped to have more control over her future. Farm life was hard, and it locked you to one place. Everyone expected that she would become a farmer's wife, but that wasn't what she wanted. For Lillian, the mindset known as the Cult of Domesticity and True Womanhood seemed too confining.

And so with exciting dreams of what might be, Lillian left home to start a new life. She taught at a country school but soon realized that didn't suit her. Drifting from job to job, town to town, she worked odd jobs. She landed work as a laundress. The hours were long, and (like teaching) the job didn't pay well. Clerking, domestic work, and factory jobs all barely put a roof over her head. Lillian discovered that there were few opportunities for women. It took all she earned to get by. This wasn't the good life, but she believed there were still options to explore.

She was ambitious and hardworking. In a telling interview with amateur historian Fred Mazzulla, Lillian suggested that being a laundress was nearly as bad as farming. "My pay was a dollar a week," she said. "My room cost fifty cents a week. There wasn't much left over." Lillian was the most diligent laundress in the establishment and was barely feeding herself. There was no money left over to buy clothes or other necessities. She asked a coworker how she managed to get by. Her fellow employee frankly told her, "I don't. . . . None of us girls do, on what they pay us." It apparently came as a surprise to this "blue-eyed" farm girl, but her fellow laundress told her that she—and most of the girls—sold their favors on the side to get by. Even more of a shock, she told Lillian they used pimps to line up their clients. The implication was that they hoped to find husbands before they got pregnant. They were trying to survive.

This hadn't been part of Lillian's game plan. In fact, it ran contrary to everything she'd been taught. However, at some point in her travels (probably in Denver), she turned to the world's oldest profession. She suggested later that the decision was a calculated choice. Tidy, thrifty, and organized, she entered into a usually disheveled profession—running, in one euphemism of the day, a "disorganized" house, but like a businesswoman. Many madams suggested that they were a step above their employees, that they didn't work on the line, but Lillian freely admitted she sold herself.

Maybe she never truly outgrew her agricultural roots, as she never enjoyed big cities or working in fancy parlor houses. She liked smaller towns, preferring her own space and some control over her daily schedule. Lillian tried performing in a dance hall, but she found that it was a lot of work. She had to be on her feet for hours at a time, which was tiring and made her ache. She also thought there was too much drinking, and she didn't like the effects of overindulging. It caused both men and women to get sloppy. The worst thing, however, was that it didn't pay well—maybe fifty cents a day—and a dancer lost most of her gratuities to the house.

Unlike many of her fallen sisters, Lillian's goal wasn't living day to day but rather planning for the future. She saved and carefully avoided the common pitfalls of the profession, specifically drugs and alcohol. Drifting westward, she saw the Great Plains—perhaps even a few of the last buffalo. She understood that it was important to follow the money, which meant capitalizing on mining strikes and boomtowns from South Dakota to Colorado.

She stopped in Denver and rented a crib on Market Street. Before she opened for business, she took the time to carefully clean and scrub her small cottage. She hung nice curtains, decorated, and made her establishment look nice. She was pleasant and bathed, and the linens were clean—not the typical desperate bawd. The "Queens of the Row" noticed her, and she quickly became friends with Mattie Silks. Occasionally she took her high-rolling callers to Mattie's House of Mirrors. Mattie offered her a job, but Lillian had other plans, plans that Mattie respected and understood.

After building her nest egg, Lillian was ready to relocate. She was eager to leave the big city and try her luck in boomtowns. The bad air, congestion, and city life in general weren't what she wanted. Perhaps she felt safer in smaller towns; her profession could be violent. At the time, working women in Denver were in a state of panic. Brutal strangulation murders had been occurring in the Tenderloin, and this was on everyone's mind. It was unsavory; little did Lillian know that she'd stepped into such a lion's den. Competition in Denver was certainly fierce, although she didn't lack for customers. She was different and more expensive, steps above so many of the callous, opium-hazed whores on the line. Her bigger concern was the high cost of doing business in Denver. Her profit margins weren't as large as she'd hoped.

Unencumbered by vices or bitterness, Lillian was able to expand. While she certainly rendered the usual services, many men found her a willing listener and paid for her time simply to have someone to talk to. Lillian was personable and nice and thus didn't lack for appointments. In today's business parlance, we'd say she recognized the importance of customer service. A client got parlor house–level treatment in a cottage. She was said to be honest and fair, which were traits she demanded from her employees when she later went into management.

Lilian made many lifelong friends. Like so many prostitutes, she wanted to keep much of her past to herself, but she did have close friends she confided in. A good example was Arthur Mink, whom she knew for decades. After her death, Mink was asked by a historian to clear up some of the details of her life and fill in the gaps. His reply was that he had promised not to talk about Lilian and wouldn't give any details.

Lillian Powers, standing, left, poses with Lillis Lovell, who owned a fancy parlor house on Denver's Market Street. PHOTOGRAPH COURTESY OF HISTORY COLORADO.

Lillian worked in Victor, Colorado, for a time, unable to find a suitable place in nearby Cripple Creek. She finally rented a crib from a boisterous drunk, a French woman named Leola Ahrens. She was euphemistically known on Poverty Row as Leo the Lion. She was a black-haired woman who had a long and checkered career in Cripple Creek. Leo had previously run a brothel and owned and leased red-light properties. Her shrewish temper and sharp tongue would make Katherine in Shakespeare's *Taming of the Shrew* seem like a choir girl. It didn't help Leo's mood any that after she rented the crib to Lillian, she suffered a reversal in finances and had to go back to brothel management full-time. As an aging woman with a love of drink, she had once run naked out of her crib. Most ignored her rants; a few miners always seemed to get her back to her cottage so she could sleep off her hangovers. In 1914, as a pathetic drunk, she was the subject of a *Collier's Magazine* article. The author wasn't impressed with Cripple Creek or Leo. At the end of the interview, Leo supposedly told him "to send some nice boys by."

Lillian cleaned up the dirty Cripple Creek cottage, refurbished it within her budget, and made it comfortable. Most cribs on the line were hastily made with pine boards. A few had windows. They were often dirty, cold, and smoky. She started doing business—and business she did. By all accounts, she turned an enviable trade. In fact, it seems she did too well, because she was taking customers away from the other girls, who complained to their landlady. When Leo noticed that Lillian was taking some of her customers, too, she started to get angry. The French woman, especially when drinking, could be mean and verbally abusive.

Lillian let her blow through her tirades, brushing them off as too much whiskey and a sour temper. But her landlady's rants became worse than usual. Her friends warned her that the madam had threatened to kill her. Lillian didn't take it seriously until one afternoon when the angry Leo exploded through Lillian's crib door with a loaded gun. Pointing it at Lillian, presumably cocking it for effect, she shouted, "You double-crossing bitch, you get out!" She threatened to kill Lillian if she didn't leave immediately.

It isn't prudent to argue with an unbalanced person who's been drinking—especially when she has a pistol aimed at your chest at point-blank range. Lillian said she'd leave on the next train. This unexpected capitulation defused Leo the Lion, who surely got the last word. Something like the cliché: "If the sun rises on you in this town, I'll kill you." Lillian said she'd be gone that evening, though she knew she could appeal to the authorities as a last-ditch effort to keep her crib. The law might help, but whore spats were a common occurrence and were mostly ignored by officials unless blood was spilled or an important citizen offended. The crazy madam might just fire her gun next time. Lillian didn't like confrontation. While business was good, Cripple Creek had lost its appeal. She booked a ticket on the night train, but before she left, Lillian thoroughly cleaned the little cottage. Never let it be said that Lillian Powers left a mess for someone else. With dignity and the help of a young boy, she lugged her baggage up the hill to the train station. In an interview before her death, Lillian said of her landlord, Leo, "She was a tough one."

Things had moved quickly, but Lillian was glad to be out of Cripple Creek; it was too wild. She wanted a quieter place to land. She called Laura Evens, who had relocated to Salida and was doing quite well. They had mutual friends but hadn't met. Lillian needed a landlord who wasn't going to shoot her for being successful. She'd heard that Laura Evens was a good landlord and knew that Laura had left Denver for many of the same reasons she had. In an interview with Mazzulla before her death in 1953, Laura Evens talked about how dangerous Denver was. She said, "Mattie Silks, when she put bars on the upper windows, her girls got scared and never recovered." Salida, at least by boomtown standards, was a quiet rail town in the southern Colorado Rockies. Laura had a good reputation. Going back to Denver would be a last resort. Lillian recalled, "I had never seen Miss Laura, but I heard about her, and I knew there was a vacancy, so I called her up. She said she had just one place left. I told her I could not come for a few days and she said it would be alright, that she would save it for me. When I got there, I offered to pay the back rent, but she wouldn't let me."

The two became good friends. Like Mattie Silks, Laura offered Lillian a place in her parlor, but Lillian politely refused. She liked her own space and felt claustrophobic in someone else's house.

She'd found a cottage in a good location and made a sound decision. It proved so profitable that Laura hired her to manage the other crib houses on her row. Within a few years, Lillian found a neighboring town—Florence, sixty-six miles to the east—to be exactly what she was looking for. Even after she moved, she and Laura remained friends and visited one another when they could.

In contrast to the rowdy mining camps and boomtowns, Florence (shown here circa 1903) was relatively stable and quiet, well suited to Lillian's demeanor and business model. PHOTOGRAPH BY LOUIS CHARLES MCCLURE, COURTESY OF DENVER PUBLIC LIBRARY WESTERN HISTORY COLLECTION, MCC-1892.

Using Laura's business model, she bought a large building near the tracks at 311 South Union Street and went to work cleaning, renovating, and making it her own. Lillian built her dream brothel—some say it cost as much as $30,000. It was a place to eat, drink, and socialize—and it happened to be a brothel. There was a dance floor, dining room, formal parlor with stylized decorations, beer garden, and hall. She had expensive furniture finished with her personal touch, as well as private living quarters for herself on the first floor. She liked diamonds and owned a diamond cross that had belonged to Mattie Silks. There was also the usual staircase leading to the private rooms.

She called it Lil's Place. She put tens of thousands of dollars into her business, and it turned out to be a good investment. Many of her railroad clients in Salida followed her to her new establishment. Florence wasn't only a railhead town but also bustled with oil companies and ore milling plants and served as a market hub for other towns nearby. Lillian could live luxuriously in a small town where business was good. There were lonely men, including soldiers leaving and coming back from World War I. In her busiest years, Lillian would have as many as ten women working for her. She also hired cooks and domestic help. Understanding the nature of a small town, Madam Lillian was discreet, having ridden the waves of the moral climate that were sweeping the country. She was a local fixture—a bit of the Old West—and knew the local politicians and townsfolk. Lillian gave to good causes and survived a number of purges.

But her business was finally closed down in the 1940s after World War II. This time, she retired for good and lived alone, apparently content, in her suite on the first floor. She continued to help with local charitable causes, including buying winter coats for children in need. On October 22, 1960, she died in a care facility, and her passing marked the last of the old line of madams, the last of her breed. She was eighty-seven. Lil's Place still stands and is now a private residence. To this day, volunteers in Florence maintain a landscaped plot called Lil's Garden on East Main Street in recognition of her generous spirit.

The Danger of Pleasure: Venereal Disease

A Night with Venus Means a Lifetime of Mercury

VENEREAL DISEASES WERE A SERIOUS OCCUPATIONAL HAZARD of prostitution. Most working women had a very good chance of catching something. Most, especially those new to the trade, worried about infection and took as much care as they could. Women in high-volume houses—and especially women who'd started to drink or use opiates—sometimes were beyond caring. Venereal disease was just another thing to endure, another reason to use drugs or drink until you were numb. When a girl found out she was infected, it was called "getting burned." She might seek medical help or try to treat herself with a bevy of remedies that ranged from harmless to lethal.

In the Old West, gonorrhea was common, as it is today. If left untreated, this bacterial disease can cause serious damage to the joints, heart, and brain. Some people develop no symptoms at all, making it that much easier to spread the disease. Gonorrhea also attacks the fallopian tubes, resulting in infertility in up to 20 percent of cases. Some prostitutes welcomed it because they wouldn't have to worry about pregnancy.

Syphilis was misunderstood and confused with gonorrhea. It's caused by a different bacterium, a spirochete. Left untreated, it progresses through four stages, which most folks in that age only partly understood. The first or primary stage appears two to four weeks after sexual contact and involves small, painless sores that can occur anywhere on the body. These can last from ten to fifty days. The secondary stage can include a rash, headache, fever, joint aches, weight loss, and extreme fatigue. It usually manifests eight weeks to seven months after infection. The rash can resemble chicken pox, which is why the disease was called the pox. In the third or latency stage, the symptoms go away, often for years, but the carrier is still highly contagious. The spirochete embeds itself in tissue and organs.

The final or tertiary stage is the most destructive. Lesions and sores again appear. The spirochete attacks the central nervous system, heart, and brain. Insanity is common at this point. As one old phrase said, "The pox got to her . . . or got to her brain."

Because so few understood syphilis in the nineteenth century, the latent stage gave rise to voodoo-like folk cures that seemed at least temporarily to work. In the 1840s, potassium iodide was said to help some patients in later stages of syphilis. Other physicians, no doubt to relieve the severity of an incredible syphilis headache, drilled into the afflicted person's skull.

Gonorrhea was often treated with copaiba balsam and ephedra, both of which have dangerous side effects. In the 1850s, Dr. John Hammond argued that ephedra was effective if used for "gonorrhea . . . in baths with warm spring water." Some practitioners used red-hot irons to cauterize chancres, including those on the genitalia. There were a number of folk remedies and mail-order cures. Some of the more common were Red Drops, Drovett's French Lunar Pills, and Unfortunate Friends. Cinnabar (a form of mercury sulfide) had been used since the 1300s. One of the most common "cures" was to take a hot steam bath and try to sweat out the poison or change one's bodily humors.

For gonorrhea, small amounts of mercury were commonly injected into men's private parts, as described so vividly in the Lewis and Clark journals: the doctor would insert a long syringe up his patient's urethra and inject a "mercury pellet." This sometimes gave relief. At the least, the operation was unpleasant and painful, making the sufferer wonder if his night with Venus was worth it.

In 1837, doctors concluded that gonorrhea and syphilis were separate diseases. This wasn't an entirely new idea. As early as the fourteenth and fifteenth centuries, physicians had suggested this. Some, like Paracelsus in the 1530s, wondered if gonorrhea might not be an early stage of syphilis. In the midst of the syphilis outbreak in the nineteenth century, some Victorian doctors wrongly thought that gonorrhea was inconsequential.

By far, the most common and probably the most effective medicine used for both gonorrhea and syphilis was mercury. The old cliché,

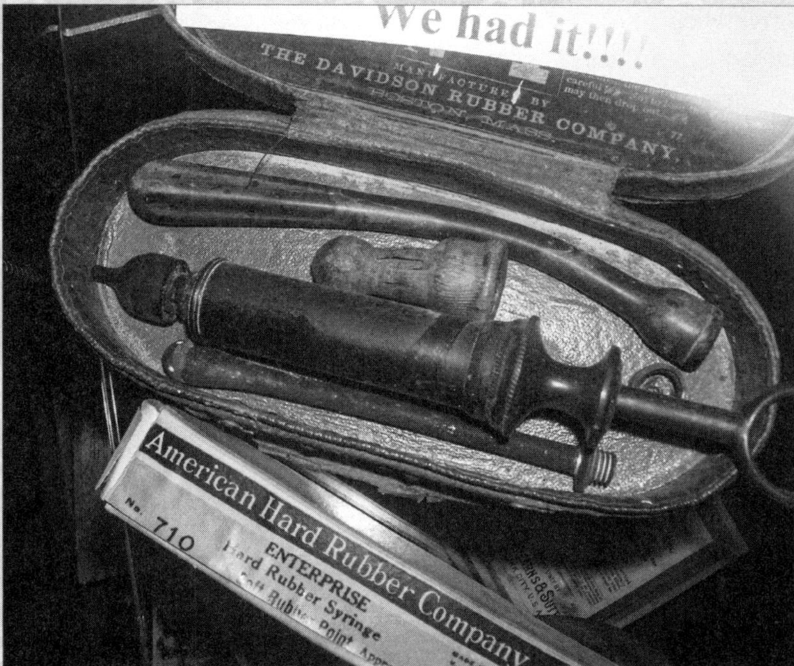

To treat venereal diseases in the 1800s, doctors used syringes like this one to inject mercury into a man's urethra. PHOTOGRAPH BY MICHAEL RUTTER.

"a night with Venus means a lifetime with Mercury," was proven time and again. The treatment could be more deadly than the disease. Mercury ointments were applied to the pox or sores in the early stages of the disease, or the victim might be coated in a mercury paste and then wrapped in a blanket; this was called the "mercury sweats." Or the doctor could simply have his patient breathe vapors of warmed mercury. The element had been prescribed for skin disorders and venereal ailments for centuries, perhaps starting with early Arabian physicians. It sometimes killed the germs in the sores, and the victim thought he or she was cured. But the disease often lurked in deeper tissues.

As we know today, mercury was a two-edged sword. It can be quite toxic, especially the vapor. In the nineteenth century, it was well known that when your gums hurt—or your teeth fell out—it was time to stop using it. Other side effects could include mouth ulcers and bleeding gums. The bones in the jaw could also be impacted, *sometimes causing gangrene. Overdose could be lethal. It wasn't uncommon for a patient to suffocate from an overdose.*

Venereal disease, particularly syphilis, had long been a scourge. In seventeenth-century Europe, nearly a quarter of the population was infected. In fact, for several centuries, the major cause of infant mortality in French hospitals was congenital syphilis. So where did this disease come from? Some have argued that the disease made its way up from Africa. Others suggested that it might have always existed but was unrecognized. Other scholars have argued that Columbus and his sailors might have brought it back to Europe from the New World. Some historians have theorized that a milder form of syphilis might have existed in Europe until a more virulent form was brought back from the New World. By 1495, the pox, as it was called, was rearing its ugly head in a very deadly way.

The flash point seemed to be when the army of Charles VIII of France besieged Naples, Italy, which was experiencing an outbreak of the pox. (As a point of interest, Columbus' crews had previously spent time in the flesh pots of Naples, and some were serving with Charles.) At any rate, the Naples whores defected to the French when it looked like the Italians would lose the battle, thus infecting the French soldiers, who in turn infected other parts of Europe. Before long, the pox was spreading across Europe like fire in a dry forest.

By the early 1500s, doctors had finally figured out that the pox was sexually transmitted. Yet it would be centuries before an effective treatment was discovered. In 1928, Scottish physician Alexander Fleming discovered penicillin and its lethal qualities against gram-positive pathogens. By 1941, scientists Howard Florey and Ernst Chain figured out how to mass produce the drug, in time for use during World War II.

11

Verona Baldwin

The Ruined Denver Madam Who Had the Last Laugh

The headline read, "A Woman's Revenge. Lucky Baldwin Shot by His Young Cousin."

The story broke on January 5, 1884, in the San Francisco Call *newspaper. Most California papers covered the story, and it made national news. Verona Baldwin told police and reporters that her cousin, multimillionaire Elias Jackson "Lucky" Baldwin, had raped her. She said, "He had defiled me and cast me aside . . . ruining my mind and body." The case went to court: Lucky versus the pretty, twenty-three-year-old, soft-spoken schoolteacher with a British accent.*

The newspapers had a field day with the story. After the alleged rape, Verona confronted Lucky on the staircase of the luxurious Baldwin Hotel in San Francisco. There, she shot him at close range. Lucky, one of the wealthiest men in California, took the bullet in the shoulder, but the wound wasn't serious.

Verona, Lucky's cousin, was employed at his Santa Anita Ranch in Arcadia, California, as a schoolteacher. "I ought to have killed him at the ranch," Verona frantically told the police on January 4, as they investigated the shooting. "I did not try and kill him. I shot just where I wanted to, for I am a good shot and never miss anything I aim at."

Lucky lived up to his trademark nickname and recovered from the gunshot. Then he fired Verona. Through his lawyer, Lucky claimed Verona's accusations of sexual assault were ludicrous and reckless. The truth, Lucky asserted, was that her behavior had been so disgusting that the house servants had complained. He said Verona had openly seduced one of his houseguests, a young doctor who was staying at the ranch while recovering from an illness. Lucky had no choice but to let his cousin go, because she wasn't fit to teach children.

Verona was jailed and charged with attempted murder. The trial became a circus, but finally she was acquitted. The publicity, though, had ruined her teaching career. Apparently, the rape resulted in a baby. It was difficult for her to find work. She tried professional acting, but that didn't pan out, and she moved out of state. Angry and reeling with frustration, she attempted to sue Lucky for child support. It was hard to get legal traction against him because he had a bevy of lawyers. However, the publicity affected his business ventures, so he used his influence with a Los Angeles judge. Verona was summoned by the court and declared insane. Then the judge committed her to an asylum in Napa, California. Verona was later released, after officials determined that she was sane and shouldn't have been sentenced.

Beaten down, Verona settled in Denver and turned from being a publicly "ruined woman" into a business model. Known as Madam Verona "Fannie" Baldwin, she ran a selective brothel on Market Street. She later shifted into legitimate business ventures and left an enviable estate upon her death in 1940. She lived to see Lucky Baldwin go broke. It gave her a great deal of satisfaction to call her successful hotel the Baldwin Inn.

The tempest made national headlines as the "he said-she said" battle played out in the press before the case ever got to a California courtroom. It was an early Christmas present for newspapers. Readers blushed but were fascinated, thus prompting a frenzy of articles. It was a perfect storm that supercharged America's fascination with rags-to-riches stories and the wiles of woebegone women, mixed with the ever-popular venue of a courtroom drama, firearms, honor, seduction, and intrigue. While Verona (who may or may not have been Lucky's cousin) admitted to shooting Lucky, her defense was that he had violated her. In that era, many courts would have acquitted her. She was also surprised that law enforcement wasn't interested in another part of her story—how she overheard Lucky making illegal land deals. This allegation was marginalized. The police had a slam-dunk case of attempted murder. Besides, officers of the law knew it was unwise to cross an important man. In the Wild West, the law often bowed to money and power.

Later, when Lucky refused to testify against Verona in open court, the prosecution's case weakened. Verona had previously done jail time, which was ugly, but winning her trial was a victory, even if the process left her destitute with—we suppose—a baby to care for. Later, when she sued for child support and ended up in a mental institution for daring to cross one of California's *nouveau riche*, Verona realized that she was a pawn in one hell of a power game.

Newspaper readers of the day wondered about her, but little was known. Details about her origins varied. She might have come from the Midwest, perhaps Indiana. She was said to be the daughter of A. J. Baldwin of Thurston County, California. At any rate, it was unfortunate that she caught the eye of Lucky Baldwin, who invited her to be a teacher on his ranch. He had a number of employees and provided a free school for their children. Now, she wasn't sure what to do. It was frightening to consider what could happen if she crossed his path again. Verona recognized that being declared insane—even though she was released with a clean bill of mental health—had discredited her.

How could she win against a man whose reach was so wide, while hers was so narrow? She knew he could hurt her in ways she couldn't imagine. Had he already thwarted her ventures in ways she hadn't been aware of? She'd tried performing on stage in San Francisco—the opportunity looked promising—but the play received bad reviews because of "her acting," so it closed. Did the tentacles of his influence reach that far? It was easy for Verona to start second-guessing as she looked at every shadow.

Much of the press about her years in California was less than flattering, if not character deflating. She was painted, at best, as an unstable woman. She wasn't someone folks wanted teaching their children in primary school. Even though Verona was legally vindicated, in her day women were either good or bad. The aspersions, unanswered questions, and doubt were damning. After all, she hadn't shown good judgment. If she had, she wouldn't have been in such a compromising situation—something all proper young girls were warned against. Innocent or not, she'd shot a man, been jailed and declared insane, had a baby, and tried to be an actress (a profession little better than being a dance hall girl); the list goes on.

There is that one lingering but unstated question: had she encouraged Lucky Baldwin? He was old enough to be her grandfather. Was Verona a trampy opportunist? The cumulative effect of these circumstantial conjectures was irreparable to her character. A piece of reportage (from the *Rocky Mountain News* on February 18, 1888) is a representative sample of the kinds of articles that were written. Her mental instability seemed to be the focus: "After her trial she was sent to an asylum . . . and was released and went to Chicago. There she was arrested for eccentric conduct, and came back to Los Angeles . . . she proved to be such a poor actress that the project fell through. The story as told by her friends is peculiar."

Occasionally, there were vindicating publications. As one example, popular author Laura Carter Holloway (in her book titled *Famous American Fortunes and the Men Who Have Made Them*) briefly described Verona in her chapter on Lucky Baldwin. This book was published in the later part of the 1880s:

> Mr. Baldwin's social life was adventurous. The incident occurred in the corridor of his hotel. The young lady was arrested and incarcerated on a charge of intent to kill. When

> the trial took place the jury was so far convinced of the truth of her story of alleged injustice and injury that she was unanimously acquitted by the verdict of "Not Guilty." Which verdict the local papers endorsed. It is evident that business capacity does not always include clarity of moral vision; did it, Mr. Baldwin's $20,000,000 would have enabled him to navigate with fewer shocks. . . . Mr. Baldwin cannot be held up in all respects as a model man.

Rags-to-riches novels celebrating the American dream were popular in the nineteenth century. Horatio Alger's novels, for example, focused on "poor lads" with strong moral values. Through hard work and diligence, these boys grew into men who were able to succeed financially without compromising their principles. Working in this genre, Mrs. Holloway lauded Baldwin's work ethic but scolded him for his flawed morality. She thought Verona had a right to defend her honor.

With no chance of redeeming herself in California, Verona decided to start fresh someplace else. She would fight another day, but it would be in another battle of another war. There were lean years, but she proved that she, too, had a mind for business.

Verona was polite, articulate, and soft-spoken. She learned that power begot power and that faith in the system may not be as useful as knowing how to use the system. Her story was well known. Consciously, discreetly, she played the part of a wronged woman. It served her well in the prostitution business. She implied that she had no other choice, since she'd been ruined by the famous Lucky Baldwin. She'd been falsely accused and thrown into a mental institution, damaging her respectability. The impression she gave was, "Ah, my, isn't it a pity. I'm a whore—but I'm a good one."

In Denver in the late 1890s, Verona saw firsthand how both Mattie Silks and Jennie Rogers used the political system to their advantage. They leveraged the corruption in the Denver Police Department and the city political machine. And while the famous madams and their machinations were slipping as Denver was trying to clean up its image, it was an object lesson learned. Verona took it a step further: it's better to use the system with the critical tools of influence and power than to fight it directly; however, political favors and fortunes aren't long-term propositions and must be constantly renegotiated.

The queens of Denver Row (aka Indian Row) had been financially successful, but they were entrenched in their institutional structures and unable to pivot effectively. Verona had a better understanding of how the world was changing, as new tides of social reform swept in. She negotiated the political and economic trends more effectively than most women in her trade. Eventually, she shifted out of the bawdy business. By the end of the century, reformers were targeting prostitution, especially the obvious and tawdry aspects of the trade. As the twentieth century unfolded, more specific laws were passed, and city ordinances became more exacting. Business practices that had been embraced and welcomed before were now public offenses, so Verona bought a luxury hotel and restaurant, which she ran until her death in 1940. She followed her cousin's career as his fortunes continued to rise and eventually fall. It would be fascinating to hear her commentary, but little direct information remains.

Elias Jackson "Lucky" Baldwin was considered a lucky man—until he wasn't. His bartender once commented, "He didn't run after women; they ran after him." His investments in mining, agriculture, business, timber, and real estate were legendary. Many parts of Southern California still bear his name. Lucky bought extensive tracts, including much of the San Gabriel Valley. He subdivided them and made a fortune. On a foreclosure, he bought 2,000 acres with a mile of lakefront property on Lake Tahoe. He developed it into a luxury resort. His Baldwin Hotel and Theatre in San Francisco was considered one of the great luxury accommodations in the world. Although he made risky investments, he made money from them, becoming one of the largest landowners in California, as well as one of the richest, most influential men in the state. When he sold his Norcross Stock on the Comstock, he made $2.5 million in profit (about $70 million in today's prices).

Lucky loved to gamble; he was especially fond of poker and horse races. He was friends with the rich and famous, including Wyatt Earp of Tombstone, Arizona. The former marshal and his common-law wife (and former prostitute), Josephine, were frequent guests at Lucky's establishments. In Josephine's memoir, *I Married Wyatt Earp*, she said that she and Wyatt were married on one of Baldwin's yachts while on a cruise. Lucky also had an expert eye for horseflesh. He had a fine collection of horses and one of the finest racetracks in the state, if not the world.

The Baldwin Hotel in San Francisco was one of Lucky Baldwin's crown jewels, and also the site where he was shot by Verona Baldwin. PHOTOGRAPH COURTESY OF THE UNIVERSITY OF CALIFORNIA–BERKELEY BANCROFT LIBRARY.

Over the years, he collected four wives—and strings of sordid affairs and broken hearts. The press made many of them public, as he was a known philanderer. After being divorced twice, he married a sixteen-year-old girl who died of consumption. Then he married another sixteen-year-old named Bennett. They separated but never divorced. He was sued by four different women that we know of—women who apparently could not be bought off. Each said he'd promised to marry her. One teenager was allegedly awarded $75,000 for breach of contract. Lucky was also sued by a certain Lillian Ashley because he seduced her. Apparently Lillian's sister later tried to shoot him in 1896 and nicked his head. Perhaps he'd grown accustomed to angry women taking shots at him. He was, again, lucky. One San Francisco paper in 1888 referred to his ranch as "Baldwin's Harem."

Lucky Baldwin entertained guests at this cottage house on a lake at his opulent ranch in Pasadena. PHOTOGRAPH BY THE DETROIT PHOTOGRAPHIC COMPANY, COURTESY OF THE LIBRARY OF CONGRESS, LC-DIG-PPMSCA-17916.

It would seem that Verona had indeed been targeted by an older man who stalked her and likely raped her. It's fair to say that Lucky was a sexual predator. He used his wealth and influence to cover up his indiscretions. The young schoolteacher Verona got her day in court, but it cost her dearly.

Lucky's long string of good luck eventually turned sour. He lost money in land speculations, and his hotel burned down. (He was lucky—again—to get out alive.) By 1898, he was land-poor and needed to become solvent. He headed north to try to reclaim his fortune in the Alaskan gold rush, but the saloon he planned to open in the Klondike didn't happen. An investment in Nome failed, and he returned home empty-handed. To make matters worse, he faced huge tax liabilities and lost most of his fortune. Baldwin's luck finally ran out on March 1, 1909, when he died at age eighty at his ranch in Arcadia.

During his lifetime, Elias Jackson "Lucky" Baldwin, shown here in 1905 at age seventy-six, certainly lived up to his nickname. PHOTOGRAPH COURTESY OF THE ARCADIA PUBLIC LIBRARY.

At the same time, in Denver, the scorned Verona was doing handsomely. If she was bitter, she didn't show it. She had a fatalistic attitude; her fate was to make money and control her future. Her old-world manners were alluring and charming. She was tall and regal and spoke with an educated English accent. She hinted that her blood was British blue. We can take her at her word, or maybe she was simply a good actress who could've played—with equal poise—Shakespeare's Lady Macbeth, Beatrice, Viola, or Portia.

Verona was considered a beautiful woman. She was fashionable and liked to wear purple velvet. She also enjoyed the colors red and gold. Her hair was thick and prematurely gray. She wore it proudly, having earned it. Many men thought it accented her hazel or green eyes (accounts differ); we can assume she had pretty eyes, no matter the color. It was rumored that she occasionally wore a tiara. She was the perfect hostess if you could afford her. Catering to the rich, her parlor was all about playing games of romance, even if the outcome was inevitable. She made a great deal of money and avoided the legal troubles that often dogged other madams.

Later descriptions of Verona Baldwin don't seem to align with those provided in the ragged and deranged newspaper accounts of her battle with Lucky. She learned the hard way that she had to make her own luck. Even after becoming a successful businesswoman in a man's world, she apparently didn't forget what it was like to have the world crash down upon her. She commanded high prices for her services, but—according to the sparse records we have—she wasn't a brutal madam or a pushover.

Being considered a fair madam was a compliment in her day. It was assumed that the madam would always get her share: around half the girl's take. It was hard for a working girl, even a highly paid parlor girl, to gain any long-term financial advantage or even to be fiscally solvent. The game was rigged in the house's favor. Debt was one of the tools that proprietors used to leverage their boarders and keep them in economic prison. Because a woman in the bawdy trade had few legal or social rights, there was little she could do but survive if the madam was vengeful. In the flesh trade, a woman was a short-term, expendable commodity. Having a fair madam was the best a woman could expect.

The competition was keen when Verona started at 2020 Market Street. She bought a luxury hotel near the state capitol and made it one of the most exclusive locations in Denver. The young girl, victimized by her cousin, had the last laugh when she called her place the Baldwin Inn.

One interesting story about Verona appeared in the *Rocky Mountain News* on April 28, 1898. It gives us another glimpse into her world. In this account, a pretty, young girl with blue eyes arrived in Denver. She was brought to see Verona by a broker who preyed on young girls.

> A woman at the employment office advised her to adopt a course of vice. . . . The woman, called "Mary Anderson,"

> in company with a notorious procuress, rang the bell of a brothel . . . the landlady was informed that the girl was innocent. . . . The landlady, Verona Baldwin . . . [told] the girl for the sake of her mother and family to return home. Verona Baldwin called the police . . . and later [the girl] was taken to Union Station.

The police made sure the young girl had a train ticket to a relative's house. Verona hadn't forgotten what it was like to be afraid, destitute, and alone.

Pregnancy

and Birth Control

*F*OR PROSTITUTES, PREGNANCY—LIKE VENEREAL DISEASE—*was an occupational hazard. Unless gonorrhea made a woman sterile, motherhood was always a possibility. And childbirth was painful and dangerous. Many women died due to obstructed deliveries, hemorrhaging, or infection. (Even today, childbirth remains risky and is the sixth most common cause of death for American women of childbearing age.) Frontier women in general prayed that they wouldn't get pregnant, as documented by a plethora of diary entries. There's no reason to assume prostitutes were any different. Most knew that sooner or later their luck could run out and they might wind up expecting. Gynecology was in its infancy and of little help, and medical information was scanty and archaic. Victorian prudishness about the human body was at its high point. Doctor visits were farcical by contemporary standards: To preserve modesty, a doctor would present a small doll. His patient would point to it to describe her symptoms. For a working woman, the income lost before and after a baby was born (with no father to provide support) was also a concern.*

A surprising number of products were designed to control or abort birth, but most were ineffectual. The French manufactured condoms, called "French Letters," made from thin skins (usually sheep gut) or vulcanized rubber. These were not very popular or widely used, although advertisements touted them for just $3 a dozen. Two popular birth-control products were Portuguese Female Pills (to prevent conception and cause abortions) and Madame Restell's Preventive Powders. Other products, often advertised in newspapers and magazines, were Yellow Dock Sarsaparilla, Henry's Invigorating Cordial, Dr. Dupanco's Golden Pills for Females, Morrell's Electro Magnetic Fluid, and Judson's Mountain Herb Pills (to remove "obstructions"). In an effort to honor Victorian sensibilities, the ads were filled with euphemisms, promising everything—in a couched and roundabout way—from birth control and abortion to menstrual pain *relief. One such euphemism was "obstacle." Again and again, one could read how this or that product would prevent or remove an "obstacle," meaning a pregnancy.*

Abortion was risky but not uncommon. One historian suggested that in some cities there might have been one abortion for every six or seven births. This number seems quite high, but many a town's Boot Hill cemetery was populated with women whose abortions went wrong. In larger towns, there were specialists; occasionally they had medical licenses. If someone in the area did abortions, the local prostitutes would know how to get in touch. After passage of the anti-obscenity Comstock Act on March 3, 1873, birth control, abortion, and other "female" product advertisements flourished, relying on euphemisms and double-talk to circumvent the law's ban on "lewd" or "lascivious" language.

12

Mae Phelps

The Modern Madam from Trinidad

*T**AKING TRINIDAD, COLORADO, BY STORM,** Mae Phelps founded the Madams' Association, established health care for prostitutes, and created a rest home for aging whores.*

Her business model would make an interesting case study in an MBA program. Mae was an entrepreneur with a progressive social conscience and a flexible, profit-driven code of ethics. She would likely be running a billion-dollar conglomerate today. Her professional organization promoted a working relationship among municipalities, law enforcement, businesses, and citizens. It helped fund bridges, roads, trolleys, and other civic improvements. Surprisingly, she even supported "sin taxes" as she organized a rather fragmented collection of disorderly houses.

Embracing a transparency that reads like a page from How Google Works, *Mae was "madam anomaly" in the prosperous mining community of Trinidad. Mae believed that segregating the sporting community into sin districts was a good idea; a cash-starved community enjoyed the revenue stream from fines, taxes, and licenses. It's interesting that Madam Mae Phelps and Carrie Nation, polar opposites, walked the same streets in the same town—each fighting for her cause, trying to win one skirmish at a time.*

Trinidad gave Carrie Nation her walking papers and fined the proselytizing prohibitionist $35 for disturbing the peace. The locals wouldn't tolerate her busting up local saloons. Nation insisted on staying in a clean place that wasn't stained by the smell of liquor. A trainman stoically said, "Ma'am, I think you got off at the wrong station. You're looking for heaven, but this is Trinidad!" As a point of cultural mythology, a resident supposedly walked up to the axe-wielding Nation and slapped her face. Crusading Carrie would dust her feet on Trinidad.

For a time, city government was at least playing that political poker game of legality and public opinion—specifically on the issues of prohibition and prostitution—buying time trying to work out the delicate balance.

In a perfunctory court appearance, Mae was officially asked by a lawyer named McKeough if she operated a disorderly house. She had a stoic sense of humor and was willing to take on city government. She retorted, "You ought to know, you've been there often enough."

Mae Phelps was one of the few businesswomen in the West who understood and reflected the changes that were occurring socially and economically during the early decades of the twentieth century in the United States—specifically in Trinidad. Having practiced her ribald trade for many years, she realized that if she didn't change, she could be swept out of business. In the early days, her profession was a shady but conspicuous part of the economy, even if it was generally referred to in euphemisms. Such sinful behavior wasn't brought up in polite or socially acceptable conversations. Mae's strategy was rather bold: she addressed the "prostitute elephant" in the room and lightly mocked the double standard. She didn't deny the metaphoric scarlet letter on her breast, but she insisted that her partners in sin—the men who paid for her services—ought to wear one, too. At least they needed to work together. Mae was one of the few who could get away with such direct honesty, because she was connected and wealthy and could afford to retire at any time. She also had a long history in the area and was respected for her business acumen. Apparently, she hadn't read Charles Eliot's handbook for respectable women called *The Ladies Repository*, in which Eliot suggested that for "the sake of good order [a woman] should submit" to a man.

Over the previous decade, sin and decency laws that regulated her business had tightened dramatically. For example, in 1911, Colorado state law made prostitution a felony. The offense not only could bring huge fines but also confiscation of personal property and up to five years in prison for the woman involved. Mae wasn't flamboyant or passive-aggressive like Laura Bell McDaniel, Laura Evens, or Mattie Silks, nor was she subtle like Verona Baldwin. She argued with logic and data, not emotion. She was forthright, listing herself as a prostitute during a public census. In a way, she was deconstructing some of the complexities and contradictions of an enforced social propriety. She rejected the occasional oversimplification of her profession as "the Great Social Evil." If pushed, she could attack the polarizing thesis that women were either good or bad—either sexless, compassionate beings just short of being angels or godless harpies who led men astray.

Most managing women in Mae's profession understood that life was hard; too many working women lived in the moment. This was one of the reasons she founded the Madams' Association. A day-to-day profession didn't lend itself to planning for the future, not even a year or five years down the line. This kind of thinking may seem obvious, but it's one of the unique differences between Mae and most of the other women featured in this book. She prepared for the future and had an action plan. She saw new waves gathering in the bay long before the swells formed. She understood the ramifications of the current political climate and planned accordingly. She probably would have supported woman's suffrage.

Mae argued for a brand of applied ethics—sometimes called utilitarian ethics—that would've made the English philosopher John Stuart Mill smile. As a catalyst for organizing the Madams' Association, she understood the importance of a collective voice. The association was not a union but a loose confederation. She built her case by

In 1913, the women of Trinidad marched in support of striking United Mine Workers, revealing an emerging belief in their own political influence. PHOTOGRAPH COURTESY OF DENVER PUBLIC LIBRARY WESTERN COLLECTION, X-60487.

stressing the benefits that prostitution gave back to the community such as taxes paid to city coffers and a contented male workforce not inclined to leave for greener pastures. Under her leadership, her associates would establish a set of rules and best practices. They would run honest houses and work with city officials whenever they could. The free-wheeling days of the Old West had passed. New, restrictive laws regarding alcohol and prostitution were sweeping the country, so a new operating model was necessary. Families, schools, and respectable businesses needed to be considered. For example, the vice district must stay isolated—out of sight, out of mind. Prostitution had to police itself and become less ostentatious. Loud and disorderly behavior could not be tolerated. This meant that overt advertising must be avoided.

Members of the Madams' Association agreed to stay on the western end of town. Patrons had to cross "The Bridge of Sighs," named after a famous bridge in Italy, to get to the red-light district. The small canyon was a natural division between the respectable and the disorderly. The association also discussed the merits of going underground—literally.

The purveyors of whiskey, women, and gambling were developing subterranean passageways. Men could slip into brothels, bars, and gambling parlors without being seen. A sporting man could go into a respectable barbershop, cigar store, or clothing establishment and then descend a staircase that led to a network of tunnels. These would take him to the pleasures of his choice. Meanwhile, the Madams' Association lobbied for and helped fund an extension of the trolley line into the vice district. This infrastructure provided a natural transition to the system of speakeasies and bootleg liquor during Prohibition. At one point, the famous gangster Al Capone effectively hid in the Trinidad underground network, eluding law enforcement.

Trinidad as it appeared in 1907. PHOTOGRAPH BY ARTHUR RUSSELL ALLEN, COURTESY OF WIKIMEDIA.

With the zeal of a revivalist, Mae promoted herself as a modern businesswoman with new ideas. She rebranded the world's oldest profession. She infused her story with altruism and precision, backed up with volumes of due diligence. Spinning a social awareness that reflected responsibility and understanding, she implied that good deeds were good business; if you believed your own sales pitch, so much the better. At the same time, she wasn't the garden-variety pushover madam whom the town council could plow over when it suited their needs. She demanded at least an honest hearing. She was, in every sense of the word, a community organizer: a madam organizing madams and representing working girls—a civic female voice, an "alternative" voice.

Mae Phelps was listed on the 1910 census and in other public records. Although she was getting older, she was still a firebrand, arguing for and trying to shape her profession, specifically through the Madams' Association. She had made a lot of money and presumably

For all of her public work in Trinidad, photographs of Mae Phelps are rare. Luckily, a local Trinidad bank clerk, Oliver E. Aultman, took the initiative when a photography shop defaulted on a loan in the late 1800s. Aultman took over the business and documented life in Trinidad in tens of thousands of images, including this one of Madam Phelps. PHOTOGRAPH BY OLIVER E. AULTMAN, COURTESY OF HISTORY COLORADO.

had begun to think about retirement. Within a few years, however, she drifted off the historical record and we mostly lose track of her. Perhaps she retired to a ranch or some home out of the public eye. In 1927, she was alleged to have had a hand in the development of the Old Madams' Home, one of her ideas that gained fruition. This home was a ranch outside of town. We know that it lasted until 1935. By then, Mae was just a memory.

That is what we know about Mae Phelps as a public figure, a lively member of the local community, and about her involvement in civic and business affairs. Unfortunately, we don't know a lot about Mae as a person or details about her private life, which was how she wanted it. It's fair to assume, though, that she knew where a lot of skeletons were buried, and that made some men nervous. Mae also knew that the Trinidad area was different from other mining areas because it centered on coal. It wasn't a boom or bust environment like a gold or silver town. Trinidad wasn't heaven, but it was far from hell if you were business-centered. She wasn't itinerant, as so many madams seemed to be. She didn't set up her parlor and have to move with every rumor of a strike. She'd built her business to last, and this was her home. Much of her career was wedded to this town. She saw it change and understood its cultural and economic history.

To understand her milieu, it helps to take a closer look. The region was steeped in tradition. There was a long and fascinating Native American history. In the 1590s, Spanish explorers visited the region. The French came later, in 1739. The Pike Expedition (1806–1807) saw one of its party killed by a marauding grizzly bear. The famous Purgatory River, which flows through the valley, was named *El Rio de Las Animas Perdidas en Purgatorio* (the River of Lost Souls) by the Spanish. The river then took on a French pronunciation and the spelling *Purgatoire*, which remains its official name. The locals later Anglicized it to Purgatory to make it easier to say. In 1846, the mountain valley was a good place to stop on the Santa Fe Trail. Later, Murdo McKenzie managed the large Matador Land and Cattle Company, and Charles Goodnight and Oliver Loving—known for the Goodnight Trail—brought thousands of cattle into the region to satisfy Colorado miners' demand for beef.

In 1872, rich deposits of coal were found, and the city exploded. Merchant Frank Bloom established the first commercial coal-mining concerns. The coal in the area was high quality, so smelters paid premium prices. Almost overnight, Trinidad became a boomtown, with coal as the new gold. By the early 1900s, more than 800 coal mines dotted the region. The inevitable cottage industries geared to meet the needs of the largely male labor force were focused on the three Ws of vice: whiskey, whoring, and wagering. Blue-collar entertainment was not afternoon tea, cutely trimmed sandwiches, and readings from the Lake Poets. These men wanted a rawboned saloon culture, spittoons, vulgarity, games of chance, and indulgent ladies. Gambling was a serious pastime. Men of the West gambled with their lives. They came to the frontier to seek fame and fortune. They would drink too much, tempt lady luck in games of chance, and maybe visit a working girl (which was, in many ways, tempting lady luck when you consider venereal disease rates). They spent what they had on sprees, escaping the cares and dangers of the mines. After the binge, they'd be hung over and go back to work deep in the earth until the next payday. Shift work meant the town was busy all day. Some men made fortunes and built huge Victorian homes on what was called Millionaire Row.

The three Ws meant rowdy and irresponsible behavior, fights, and misunderstandings, often resolved with fists, guns, and knives. When men came to town for a bender, it was called "cutting the wolf loose" for a reason. Someone had to keep the peace while miners, fueled by excessive amounts of alcohol, fought and played and lost their money. Towns needed serious peacekeeping, so they hired men with fearsome reputations. Bat Masterson, for instance, was employed to tame Trinidad as an official deputy. Never mind if he got a little drunk now and then and shot out a few streetlights. On one occasion, he was joined by a few of his rowdy friends: the Earp boys and a tubercular Doc Holliday. After their thirty-second shootout at the O.K. Corral in Tombstone, Arizona, they needed a place to lie low. They were tough men, hellraisers, gamblers, and panderers. Whether someone was labeled a lawman or an outlaw often depended on who had a badge pinned to his chest. While lawmen were paid to uphold the law, they could choose to enforce it selectively.

Mae was familiar with Trinidad's wild side and certainly knew many of the more colorful men personally and professionally. This was a big part of her world, and a seasoned Mae would have learned when to duck and when to be defensive. She survived and prospered for decades in a volatile—if not violent—business climate. She had to play both sides of the street, because anyone with money could be her client. That included the miner, sheriff, gunman, outlaw, politician, and mine owner.

Fights were an everyday occurrence. The most famous shootout in Trinidad occurred in the spring of 1882. It involved "Cockeyed" Frank Loving and John Allen, both gamblers with an affinity for working ladies. But Loving was known as a *bad* man, meaning he was a "tough"—a good man with a gun or fists but a bad man to tangle with. He was a longtime friend of Masterson and the Earps from their Dodge City days. Loving and Allen had a long-standing grudge. After a shouting match, they cooled down, but then they got back into another fight. Both had been drinking. This time, they exchanged shots and missed; fortunately, no bystanders took their stray rounds. They played a deadly game of cat and mouse around town, shooting and missing. Loving ran out of shells and entered a hardware store. Allen saw his advantage and plugged Loving in the back. It took Loving a few days to die. Allen was charged with murder but was acquitted at trial because Loving had a reputation and Allen didn't believe he would've had a chance in a fair fight. (Allen changed his wandering ways and went on to become a preacher.)

The psychotic gunman Clay Allison also passed through Trinidad occasionally. According to rumor, he had a few "personal plumbing problems" from one too many visits with lewd women. He was reportedly treated by Trinidad doctors, who apparently had a lot of experience trying to cure social diseases. The town also saw the likes of Billy the Kid and members of the Wild Bunch. Thomas "Black Jack" Ketchum haunted the area and was a friend of Butch Cassidy and his Fort Worth Five. He often hid near Trinidad and occasionally came to town to enjoy the "high-class" sins of the flesh. Of course, this kind of entertainment took a lot of money, but Black Jack was a train robber—as it turns out, not a good one. He took a bullet and lost his arm, but the amputation healed nicely, so he was hanged in the spring of 1901. The hangman was apparently inexperienced and used a rope that was too long. Black Jack was decapitated, but they sewed his head back on. (You can read more about him in my book *Outlaw Tales of Utah*.)

There weren't enough experienced miners, so mining companies sought to recruit men from Europe. Large populations of Germans, Scandinavians, Italians, Slavs, and Greeks answered. They formed small ethnic communities within Trinidad. These miners were promised a new land, a nice place to live, competitive wages, and safe mining conditions. As a rule, they got one out of four: a chance to make something of themselves in America. Wages were low, housing was bad, and mining conditions were abysmal. In fact, safety conditions were worse than the mines they'd left in the Old Country. Locally, mining accidents occurred at a rate more than double the national average; a risky occupation had become incredibly dangerous. Colorado passed mine-safety laws, but mine owners refused to comply. They argued that they couldn't afford to. This led to further frustrations. Attempts by labor to organize were quickly and brutally quelled, culminating in the Ludlow Massacre of the Colorado Coalfield War, about twenty miles from Trinidad. The Ludlow mine was operated by the Colorado Fuel and Iron Company (CF&I), which was owned by billionaire John D. Rockefeller, Jr. To break the union, he called up his buddy, the governor of Colorado, who brought in the Colorado National Guard. There was pushing and shoving on both sides. On April 20, 1914, soldiers opened fire on 1,200 striking miners armed with shovels and picks. At least twenty-five people were killed, including women and children. This led to other incidents, and nearly 200 people would die before the union movement was broken by the end of the year.

Between 1870 and 1900, Trinidad saw tremendous industrial growth, mirroring growth in the state and nation. The frontier had been tamed and its natural resources leveraged. Mark Twain satirically called this the Gilded Age, a time when serious social problems were masked by a thin layer of great wealth. Despite the occasional economic panic, some men amassed unbelievable fortunes by developing (and often monopolizing) railroad, mining, and manufacturing empires. For example, John D. Rockefeller, the world's first billionaire (equivalent to about $30 billion today), held assets equal to 1.5 percent of the nation's total economic output. Morgan, Guggenheim, Mellon, Carnegie, and Goud—to name a handful—were among the financial giants known by history as robber barons. Many had deep roots and made their millions in Colorado.

At the same time, a large middle class was emerging and taking political shape. Wages were higher in the United States than in Europe, and there were opportunities never dreamed of in the Old Country. Wages in the U.S. industrial sector had risen nearly 50 percent, from $380 a year in 1880 to $565 by 1899. There was land to be settled and developed as the American dream was chased and sometimes realized. Prosperity was determined not by royal bloodlines but by work ethic and drive.

Yes, there was still poverty, inequality, and pretense, but the age was flavored with hope. New voices were being heard, voices that were shaping the democratic process. There was a heightened awareness of the human condition. Free enterprise provided opportunities for wealth and development, but society also had a responsibility to take care of itself. Corruption was being called out. Reform had many faces: antitrust laws, federal reserves, eight-hour workdays, child-labor laws, unions, collective bargaining, and industrial safety measures. There were trends toward human rights, women's rights, and prohibition. A redefining of nationalism was dawning as the United States became a world power. After the near extinction of the buffalo, environmental preservation became a consideration. Many of these philosophies found fertile ground during the presidency of Theodore Roosevelt.

Colorado was a land of rich natural resources, but it lacked capital. East Coast investors, as well as investors from Europe, controlled many of the large industries. While the investment was a blessing, it could also be a curse. A hiccup on the East Coast could have ripple effects in the Rocky Mountains. Like many Western towns, Trinidad faced a serious intersection and wasn't sure how to navigate the new winds. The hellraising young town needed to mature. But how did you shed your wicked image and instead become nice, reformed, and proper? Politicians and business owners had one foot in an amalgamation of church socials, political correctness, and high teas, where you had to decide which spoon to use for your soup and how to hold your tea cup; the other foot was in the whorehouses, where they played poker and three-card monte, drank beer and shots, and watched the tempting girls.

By 1910, gambling was illegal in every state. Mae couldn't change national trends, but she understood local businessmen. She knew the city fathers liked to hang on to their money. They loved the concept of self-government—especially government that could pay for itself with limited taxation or without increasing fees for business licenses. Mae argued for her version of sin-driven, trickle-down economics: let vice, in a decriminalized manner, pay for social causes. They forged reciprocities and working agreements. They kept reformers at bay, at least for a time. Mae understood that Trinidad needed at least to appear to be socially responsible.

By 1912, the *Titanic* had sunk; future U.S. president Ronald Reagan was crawling in his parents' living room; FDR was serving in the New York state senate; and 10 percent of Trinidad's operating budget was still coming from taxes and fines on prostitution in the red-light district. Madam Mae argued that she and her Madams' Association could make a civic difference. They'd go on to fund a spur for the town trolley. (Of course, it would end up in the red-light district, which was good for her business, but never mind the details.) She'd also pay, or help pay, for other civic improvements. At the same time, she proposed health care to curb the spread of venereal disease. While she was at it, she thought, why not build a rest home for old whores so they wouldn't have to walk the streets with canes and hearing aids?

In the end, though, the national reform movement was overwhelming, reaching even Trinidad and forcing Mae into retirement.

Mae Phelps was a savvy businesswoman and shrewd surveyor of social trends. PHOTOGRAPH BY OLIVER E. AULTMAN, COURTESY OF HISTORY COLORADO.

Bibliography

ABBOTT, Edith. *Women in Industry: A Study in American Economic History.* D. Appleton and Co., 1910.

ALDRIDGE, Dorothy. *Historic Colorado City: The Town with a Future.* Little London Press, 1996.

ANDERSON, Amanda. *Tainted Souls and Painted Faces: The Rhetoric of Fallenness in Victorian Culture.* Cornell University Press, 1993.

ARMITAGE, Susan, and Elizabeth Jameson, eds. *The Women's West.* University of Oklahoma Press, 1987.

BANCROFT, Caroline. *Six Racy Madams of Colorado.* Bancroft Booklets, 1965.

BILLINGTON, Ray Allen. *America's Frontier Heritage.* Holt, Rinehart, and Winston, 1966.

BIRD, Allan G. *Bordellos of Blair Street: The Story of Silverton, Colorado's Notorious Red Light District.* Packrat Publishing, 1993.

BLAIR, Edward, and E. Richard Churchill. *Everybody Came to Leadville.* Timberline Books, 1971.

BLAIR, Edward. *Leadville: Colorado's Magic City.* Fred Pruett Books, 1980.

BROWN, Dee Alexander. *The Gentle Tamers: Women of the Old Wild West.* Bantam Pathfinder Editions, 1974.

BROWN, Robert L. *Colorado Ghost Towns Past and Present.* Caxton Press, 1981.

BULLOUGH, Vern. *The History of Prostitution.* University Books, 1964.

BUTLER, Anne M. *Daughters of Joy, Sisters of Misery: Prostitutes in the American West 1865–90.* University of Illinois Press, 1987.

Butler, Anne M., and Ona Siporin. *Uncommon Common Women: Ordinary Lives of the West.* Utah State University Press, 1996.

Clarke, E.H. "Sex in Education; or, A Fair Chance for Girls." Project Gutenberg, 2006. http://www.gutenberg.org/files/18504/18504-h/18504-h.htm

Clemens, Samuel L. (Mark Twain). *Roughing It.* Harper & Brothers, 1899.

Darley, George Marshall. *Pioneering in the San Juan.* Fleming H. Revell Company, 1895.

Dary, David. *Seeking Pleasure in the Old West.* University Press of Kansas, 1995.

Day, James, et al. *Women of Texas.* Texan Press, 1972.

Dial, Scott. *Saloons of Denver.* The Old Army Press, 1973.

Dichamp, Christiane Fischer, ed. *Let Them Speak for Themselves: Women in the American West, 1849–1900.* Archon Books, 1977.

DiLorenzo, Thomas J. "The Culture of Violence in the American West: Myth Versus Reality," *Independent Review* 15, no. 2 (Fall 2010): 227–240.

Dodds, Joanne West. *What's a Nice Girl Like You Doing in a Place Like This?* Focal Plain, 1996.

Finnegan, Frances. *Poverty and Prostitution: A Study of Victorian Prostitutes in York.* Cambridge University Press, 1979.

Ford, John. *The Man Who Shot Liberty Valance.* Paramount Pictures, 1962.

General Assembly of the State of Colorado, *Nuisances Houses of Prostitution: An Act Concerning Nuisances, and Providing Penalties and Procedure with Relation Thereto*, April 12, 1915, Senate Bill 88, Ch.123, 360–363.

Gray, James H. *Red Lights on the Prairies.* Signet, New American Library, 1971.

GRISWOLD, Don L., and Jean Harvey Griswold. *History of Leadville and Lake County, Colorado: From Mountain Solitude to Metropolis,* vol. 2. Colorado Historical Society, 1996.

HALLER, John, and Robin Haller. *The Physician and Sexuality in Victorian America.* W. W. Norton and Company, 1974.

HAPKE, Laura. *Girls Who Went Wrong: Prostitutes in American Fiction, 1885–1917.* Bowling Green State, 1989.

HINE, Robert V. *The American West: An Interpretive History.* Little, Brown and Company, 1973.

HINE, Robert V., and John Mack Faragher. *Frontiers: A Short History of the American West.* Abridged ed. Yale University Press, 2008. University of California Press, 1993.

HOBSON, Barbara Meil. *Uneasy Virtue: The Politics of Prostitution and the American Reform Tradition.* University of Chicago Press, 1987.

HORAN, James. *Desperate Women.* G. P. Putnam's Sons, 1952.

HUNT, Inez, and Wanetta W. Draper. *To Colorado's Restless Ghosts.* Sage Books, 1960.

HUNTER, J. Marvin, ed. *The Trail Drivers of Texas.* Cokesbury Press, 1925.

HURTADO, Albert L. "When Strangers Met: Sex and Gender on Three Frontiers." In *Writing the Range: Race, Class, and Culture in the Women's West,* Elizabeth Jameson and Susan H. Armitage, eds. University of Oklahoma Press, 1997.

JEFFREY, Julie. *Frontier Women: "Civilizing" the West? 1840–1880.* Macmillan, 1998.

JENSEN, Joan M., and Darlis A. Miller. "The Gentle Tamers Revisited: New Approaches to the History of Women in the American West." *Pacific Historical Review* 49, no. 2 (May 1, 1980): 173–213.

JOHNSON, Susan Lee. *Roaring Camp: The Social World of the California Gold Rush.* W. W. Norton and Company, 2000.

KESSLER-HARRIS, Alice. *Out to Work: A History of Wage-Earning Women in the United States.* Oxford University Press, 1982.

LAMAR, Howard R., ed. *The Reader's Encyclopedia of the American West.* Thomas Y. Crowell Publishers, 1977.

MACKELL, Jan. *Brothels, Bordellos, and Bad Girls: Prostitution in Colorado, 1860–1930.* University of New Mexico Press, 2004.

MACKELL, Jan. *Red Light Women of the Rocky Mountains.* University of New Mexico Press, 2009.

MAZZULLA, Fred. Manuscript Collection, MSS 1881, Box 84, Transcripts of Laura Evens, History Colorado, February 6, 2016.

MAZZULLA, Fred, and Jo Mazzulla. *Brass Checks and Red-Lights.* Privately published, 1966.

MCLOUGHLIN, Denis. *Wild and Woolly: An Encyclopedia of the Wild West.* Barnes and Noble, 1975.

MILLER, Max, and Fred Mazzulla. *Holladay Street.* Ballantine Books, 1962.

MILLER, Stuart Creighton. *The Unwelcome Immigrant: The American Image of the Chinese, 1784–1882.* University of California Press, 1969.

O'NEAL, Bill. *Encyclopedia of Western Gunfighters.* University of Oklahoma Press, 1979.

RILEY, Glenda. *The Female Frontier: A Comparative View of Women on the Prairie and the Plains.* University Press of Kansas, 1988.

RILEY, Glenda, and Richard W. Etulain, eds. *Wild Women of the Old West.* Fulcrum Publishing, 2003.

ROGERS, Daniel T. *Atlantic Crossings: Social Politics in a Progressive Age.* Belknap Press, 1998.

ROSEN, Ruth. *The Lost Sisterhood: Prostitution in America, 1900–1918.* Johns Hopkins University Press, 1982.

RUTTER, Michael. *Bedside Book of Bad Girls.* Farcountry Press, 2008.

RUTTER, Michael. *Boudoirs to Brothels: The Intimate World of Wild West Women.* Farcountry Press, 2014.

RUTTER, Michael. *Myths and Mysteries of the Old West,* 2nd ed. Two Dot Press, 2005.

RUTTER, Michael. *Outlaw Tales of Utah,* 2nd ed. Two Dot Press, 2011.

RUTTER, Michael. *Upstairs Girls: Prostitution in the American West.* Farcountry Press, 2005.

RUTTER, Michael. *Wild Bunch Women.* Two Dot Press, 2003.

SCHARNHORST, Gary. *Bret Harte: Opening the American Literary West.* University of Oklahoma Press, 2000.

SEAGRAVES, Anne. *Soiled Doves: Prostitution in the Early West.* Wesanne Publications, 1994.

SECREST, Clark. *Hell's Belles: Prostitution, Vice and Crime in Early Denver,* rev. ed. University Press of Colorado, 2002.

SHANNON, William. *The American Irish.* Macmillan, 1963.

SHOWALTER, E. *The Female Malady: Women, Madness, and English Culture 1830–1980.* Pantheon Books, 1985.

SMITH, Duane A. *Sisters in Sin: The Nellie Spencer Story.* Western Reflections Publishing Company, 2011.

SNELL, Joseph. *Painted Ladies of the Cowtown Frontier.* Kansas City Posse of the Westerners, 1965.

STEVENS, J. David. "'She War a Woman': Family Roles, Gender, and Sexuality in Bret Harte's Western Fiction." *American Literature* 69, no. 3, 1997.

TURNER, Frederick J. *The Significance of the Frontier in American History.* University of Microfilms, Inc., 1966.

VALENTI, Jessica. *The Purity Myth: How America's Obsession with Virginity Is Hurting Young Women.* Seal Press, 2009.

WALKOWITZ, Judith R. *Prostitution and Victorian Society: Women, Class, and the State.* Cambridge University Press, 1982.

WEST, Elliot. *The Saloon on the Rocky Mountain Mining Frontier.* University of Nebraska Press, 1979.

WHITE, Richard. *"It's Your Misfortune and None of My Own": A History of the American West,* 1st ed. University of Oklahoma Press, 1991.

WOMMACK, Linda R. *Our Ladies of the Tenderloin: Colorado's Legends in Lace.* Caxton Press, 2005.

WORSTER, Donald. "Beyond the Agrarian Myth." In *Trails: Toward a New Western History,* Patricia Nelson Limerick, Clyde A. Milner II, and Charles E. Rankin, eds., 3–25. University Press of Kansas, 1991.

WRIGHT, Robert. *Dodge City, The Cowboy Capital.* Published by the author, 1913.

Index

Page numbers in **bold** indicate images.

D

E

O

P

Q

R

About the Author

MICHAEL RUTTER is a recipient of the Ben Franklin Book Award for Excellence and the Rocky Mountain Book Publishers' Award. A self-proclaimed "addict" of fly fishing, he has seen his outdoor essays published by such eminent and well-known entities as Yale University and *Outdoor Life*. He worked with American Experience on "The Wild West Series," *Butch Cassidy and the Sundance Kid*. He has been a Christa McAuliffe Fellow and an AT&T Scholar.

His books on Western themes include *Upstairs Girls: Prostitution in the American West; Boudoirs to Brothels: The Intimate World of Wild West Women; Myths and Mysteries of the Old West; Wild Bunch Women; Outlaw Tales of Utah; Bedside Book of Bad Girls: Outlaw Women of the American West;* and *Utah Off the Beaten Path.*

More Stories of the West

from FARCOUNTRY PRESS

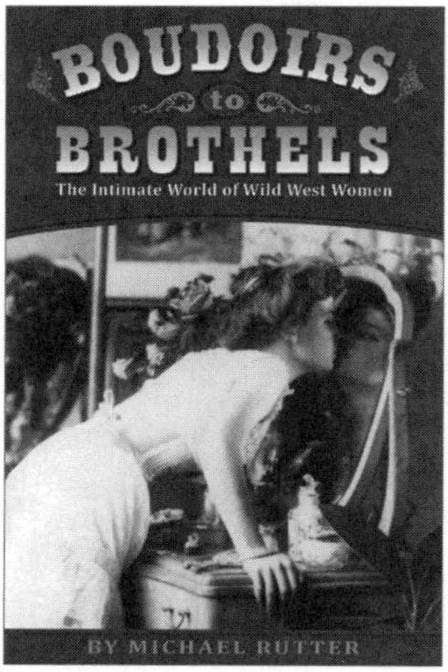

Boudoirs to Brothels:
The Intimate World of Wild West Women

By Michael Rutter

Enter the intimate world of the Wild West's women of the night. Eighteen richly researched biographies of prostitutes and madams reveal the tricks and torments of the trade.

Upstairs Girls:
Prostitution in the American West

By Michael Rutter

Historian Michael Rutter offers a thorough and fascinating history on these women for hire—including details on what their lives were like and why they turned to the profession.

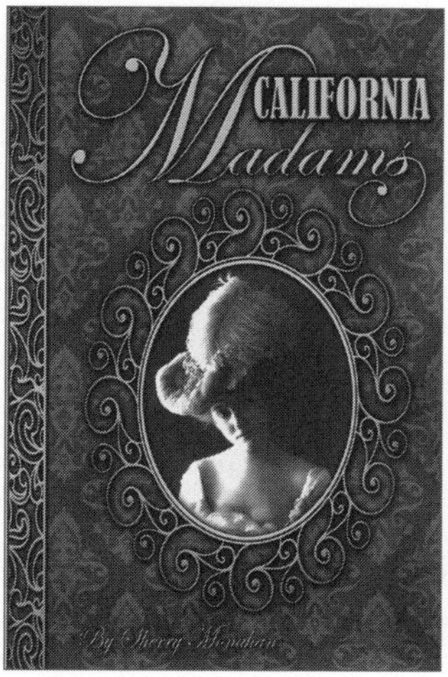

California Madams

By Sherry Monahan

Rich in details combed from historical archives, California Madams uncovers the enigmatic and salacious lives of twenty-four women who ran houses of ill repute in the Land of Sunshine and Opportunity from the 1840s to the 1940s.

Idaho Madams

By Milana Marsenich

Idaho Madams uncovers the mysterious and scandalous lives of women who ran houses of ill repute that had a role in shaping many communities in the Gem State. Author Milana Marsenich introduces these characters in a lively, easy-to-read collection that draws on the historical record to provide context for these women's lives.

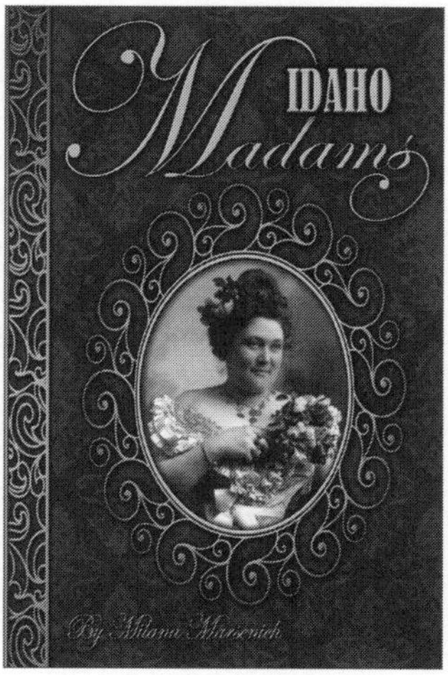

Montana Madams

By Nann Parrett

With painstaking research and rare historical photographs, Nann Parrett uncovers the complex lives of twenty-three madams under the Big Sky from the 1860s into the 1980s.

Bad Boys of the Black Hills
...and Some Wild Women, Too

By Barbara Fifer
Introduction by Jerry Bryant
of the Adams House Museum

Welcome to the 1880s Black Hills, where you will meet a host of rowdies, ranging from tall-tale tellers to killers, such as robber "Laughing Sam" Hartman or killer "Persimmon Bill" Chambers.

Bedside Book of Bad Girls:
Outlaw Women of the American West

By Michael Rutter

Profiles twenty-one of the West's gun-slinging bad girls. Meet these fascinating characters, complete with their pistols and petticoats, their knives and knaves, their vices and victims.

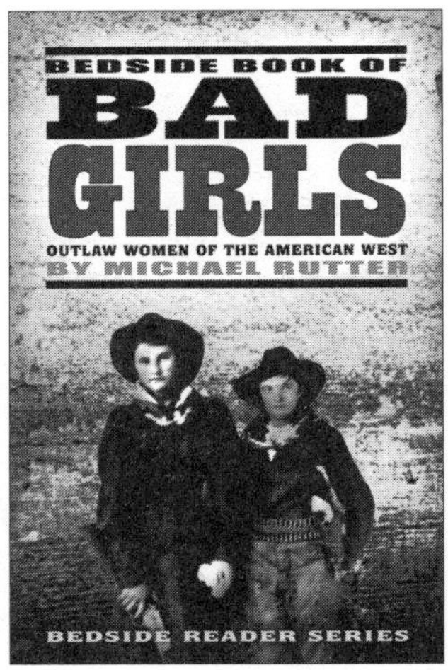

Bedside Book of Bad Girls:
Outlaw Women of the Midwest

By Chris Enss

Fascinating tales of outlaw women in the Midwest. Meet Kate King, secret courier during the Civil War and once the most wanted woman in the U.S.; Victoria Claffin Woodhull, political radical and the first female candidate for President of the United States; and many more fascinating characters of the late nineteenth and early twentieth centuries.

Deadwood Saints and Sinners

By Jerry L. Bryant and Barbara Fifer

Discover the true Deadwood! Authors Bryant and Fifer have mined the archives for obscure (and true!) tales of murderous women, artful con men, woebegon children, and more.

Deadwood's Al Swearingen

Manifest Evil in the Gem Theatre

By Jerry L. Bryant and Barbara Fifer

You've followed his wicked misdeeds and cuss-filled rants on the HBO series *Deadwood*, now go inside the life and death—of the real Al Swearingen.

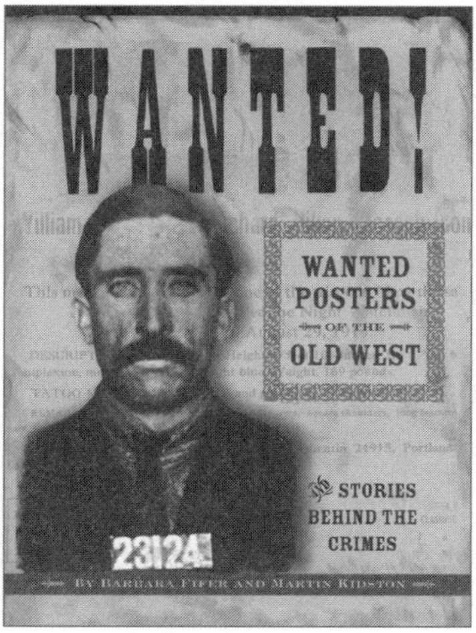

Wanted!

Wanted Posters of the Old West

Text by Barbara Fifer and Martin J. Kidston

A rare collection of more than 140 wanted posters and reward notices—and the fascinating stories behind many of the crimes. Posters for notorious bandits such as Jesse James, Butch Cassidy, and the Sundance Kid.

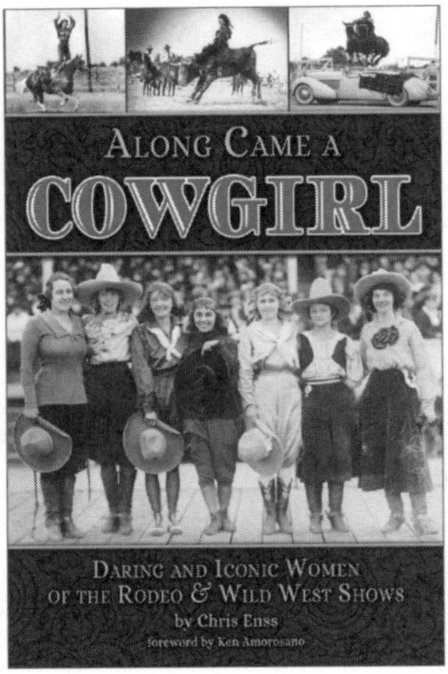

Along Came a Cowgirl:
Daring and Iconic Women of Rodeos and Wild West Shows

By Chris Enss

Best-selling author Chris Enss introduces you to the world of early rodeo—and to the stories of the women whose names resounded in rodeo arenas across the nation in the early twentieth century. These cowgirls dared to break society's traditional roles in the male dominated rodeo and trick riding world, defying all expectations.

Lady Long Rider:
Alone Across America on Horseback

By Bernice Ende

Accompanied only by her horses and an exceptional dog named Claire, Bernice Ende has logged more than 30,000 miles in the saddle, crisscrossing North America. This incredible memoir chronicles her life on the road.

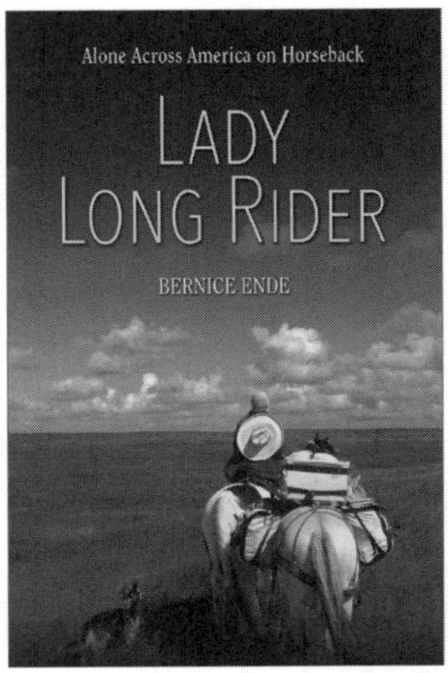

A Woman's Way West:
In and Around Glacier National Park, 1925-1990

By John Fraley

Doris Ashley left her Iowa farm in 1925 after a string of personal tragedies, riding the train west to Glacier National Park. This is her story—her love affair with the wild Crown of the Continent, the rugged landscape, and equally rugged inhabitants. Romance, grit, and wit abound.

GLACIER NATIONAL PARK:
THE FIRST 100 YEARS

By C. W. Guthrie
Published in partnership with the Glacier National Park Conservancy

Guthrie details the remarkable geologic and human history of this unmatched and storied land, then profiles Glacier National Park decade by decade.

ROCKY MOUNTAIN NATIONAL PARK:
IN AND AROUND THE FIRST 100 YEARS

Text by Mary Taylor Young

Award-winning author Mary Taylor Young celebrates Rocky's centennial with a grand story that begins when the mountains were young and continues through the dramatic flood of 2013 and into the future.